Making Stained Glass Lamps

Michael Johnston

Photographs by Alan Wycheck

STACKPOLE BOOKS

0 11557 03613 8

Published by
STACKPOLE BOOKS
5067 Ritter Road
Mechanicsburg, PA 17055
www.stackpolebooks.com

Printed in China

10 9 8 7 6 5 4 3 2 1

First edition

Cover design by Tessa J. Sweigert

Library of Congress Cataloging-in-Publication Data

Johnston, Michael, 1947–
  Making stained glass lamps / Michael Johnston ;
photographs by Alan Wycheck. — 1st ed.
    p. cm.
  ISBN-13: 978-0-8117-3613-8
  ISBN-10: 0-8117-3613-X
  1. Glass craft—Patterns. 2. Glass painting and stain-
ing—Patterns. 3. Glass lampshades. I. Title.
TT298.J654   2010
  749'.63—dc22
                                    2009021081

contents

acknowledgments

This book is dedicated to the thousands of students who have taken classes in our studio over the past twenty-four years. The myriad questions that they posed and the issues they encountered helped us develop and refine teaching programs aimed at ensuring success in the craft.

As the planning for *Making Stained Glass Lamps* began to unfold, I realized that many people would lend an important hand in its development.

I thank Mark Allison and Janelle Steen from Stackpole Books for their patience and expert guidance from the conceptualization of the project clear through to the final product.

Thanks to photographer Alan Wycheck for his keen ability to see things most people miss and then capture them with his Nikon.

Much appreciation goes out to my loyal friends at Rainbow Vision Stained Glass: Lynn Haunstein, Nan Maund, and Lee Summers. In addition to contributing designs and samples for the Stained Glass Lamp Gallery, they all ably assisted in many aspects of the book's production.

Melissa Flood, my older daughter and data entry expert, interpreted my hieroglyphics accurately and entered them into the computer. Ashley Johnston, my honors English whiz kid, provided a stellar first-round editing. Craig Johnston, my firstborn, father of two and soon-to-be forty, provided some sound advice regarding the book's final form. All in all they are three great kids!

Last, I thank Jane, my wife for the last twenty-five years. Her encouragement and assistance, as well as her willingness to forego lots of fun family time, helped immensely. She's the best!

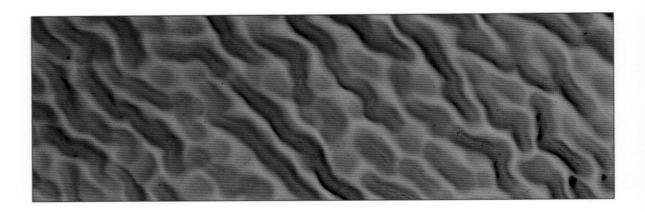

iv

introduction

Shortly after the invention of the incandescent bulb, stained glass lampshades were being created to light the fancier homes in the country. Taking flat pieces of glass and fashioning them into three-dimensional objects was not only a revolutionary concept, but it also opened a door to a more functional side of the craft.

In this book, we have provided you with two different designs and complete step-by-step details for making your own lampshade. The 20-inch shade is large enough to hang over a dining room table or a bar but can just as easily be displayed on a large table or floor base.

A project of this magnitude is not meant for a novice stained-glass crafter. However, we have included detailed primers in glass cutting and soldering. We have also provided a flat panel design to complete as practice. Once your glass is separating cleanly along your score line and your solder seams are round and smooth, you will be ready to start your lamp.

As you work through the lamp project, you will learn advanced cutting and foiling techniques as well as the proper use of a lamp leveler and bracing blocks. You will also learn how to tin a vase cap and attach reinforcing wire. Procedures for building the lamp's cone, attaching the skirt, and soldering all connections will also be detailed. Chapter 7 includes stained glass repair instructions in the event that you break a piece or two of glass along the way.

While all of the ideas and procedures presented here are intended to facilitate the successful completion of your lampshade, you will be developing skills that will allow you to complete almost any other shade. So be patient. Read all of the instructions and refer back to the cutting and soldering primers if you need to.

As you are building your lamp, if you have questions or comments about this book, please contact us through our website (www.rainbow-visionsg.com). We will make every effort to send you a response. And when your shade is finished, be sure to send us a photograph of your masterpiece so we can add it to our Internet gallery.

Are you ready to begin? Let's get started!

A Good Work Environment

A S YOUR INTEREST IN STAINED GLASS BLOS-
soms, you will soon discover that you are spend-
ing a great deal of time in your glass shop. Four
elements contribute to a comfortable and efficient
working environment.

- good light source
- sturdy work table
- nearby water source
- adequate ventilation

All aspects of stained glass making (cutting, foiling,
soldering, and so on) involve a need for precision, and
the better you see, the better the final product will be.
A two- or four-bulb fluorescent light hanging over a
workbench is generally adequate.

A work table should be sturdy and at a height comfortable for the user. If you are of average height, a
tabletop approximately 34 inches from the floor will
probably work well. Plywood construction is ideal, and
a size of 30 inches by 72 inches will handle most projects. The gray-colored work surface shown here is a
piece of fire-resistant Homasote about 2 feet by 3 feet in
size that can be placed on the plywood.

stained glass supply stores. You can also experiment with opening adjacent doors and windows to create a cross breeze in your work area.

In addition to the shop features previously listed, several other items will be very useful:

- bench brush and dustpan for cleaning up glass shards and other debris
- storage bins for sheets of glass
- cabinet for chemicals and tools
- comfortable stool
- radio or CD or MP3 player
- multi-receptacle surge suppressor with LED light for operating several electrical items at once (the light will act as a visual reminder to turn off your soldering iron at the end of each work session).

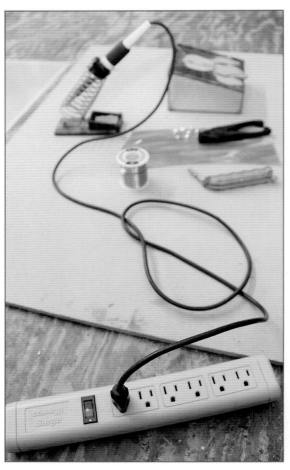

Homasote has a firm surface with a slight spring, which makes it perfect for glass cutting. (Plywood by itself is a bit rigid.) Pins and nails are easily secured in Homasote, and soldering is easier and safer due to its fire resistance. Homasote used to be readily available at all building supply stores but is no longer as common. You might have to call around to find it or settle for a substitute product.

In addition to providing the crafter with a handy place to wash up, a nearby sink will make it easy to clean the project at several stages. Any size basin can work, but one with an opening 12 inches by 20 inches or larger is ideal. Plan to use a screen strainer to prevent sand and other debris from making their way into your drainpipes.

Set up a shop in an area that is convenient to you based on what rooms you have available. You will only have so many options, and often you do the best you can with your space. Ideally, you will want a room with good ventilation so air can move through your work area during the soldering stage. If this type of setup is not possible, use a small table fan on your work table or purchase a smoke absorber, which is available at

STAINED GLASS SAFETY

Stained glass making is generally a very safe craft, and by adopting the safety precautions listed here, you will greatly reduce the likelihood of injuries and health problems.

- The most common injury that occurs in crafting stained glass is a cut finger. Prevention includes careful handling of the glass and frequent brushing of your work area to eliminate shards and specks of glass.
- If you do get a cut, tend to it immediately by applying an antiseptic and adhesive bandage. Keep these items at close hand in your shop.
- Never eat, drink, or smoke while engaged in any of the steps in making stained glass items.
- Be careful and use common sense when working with lead cames and solder. Generally, stained glass crafters are exposed to only very low levels of lead while building their projects. Make sure to bandage any open wounds and thoroughly wash your hands after working with lead or solder.
- Wear closed-toed shoes at all times to avoid glass injuries to your feet.
- Do not allow children or pets in your work area.
- Wear rubber gloves when working with patinas and etching cream. These substances can cause chemical burns on exposed skin and be harmful if absorbed into the bloodstream.
- Always wear safety goggles when cutting or grinding glass.
- Use care when handling large sheets of glass. Grip the sheet by its top edge and move it slowly to avoid jarring. Never hold a large sheet of glass horizontally because it might crack from the strain. Never try to catch a falling sheet of glass—let it go and move quickly out of the way.
- To avoid burns, use a heavy-duty stand to hold your soldering iron when not in use.
- Take care that the cord of the soldering iron does not become entangled in the spirals of the stand; otherwise, the cord may be damaged and electrical problems may occur.
- When soldering, position your head so that you are not directly breathing in fumes from the flux.
- Always wash your hands thoroughly after working in any phase of stained glass construction.
- Avoid soldering in tight spaces with little ventilation. Create airflow with a small fan or open windows. Smoke absorbers (shown below) are also available in most stained glass supply shops.

- Consider placing a piece of rubber-backed carpet under your work area. It will provide a comfortable cushion to stand on and can rescue any pieces of glass that find their way to the floor.

2

Equipment and Materials

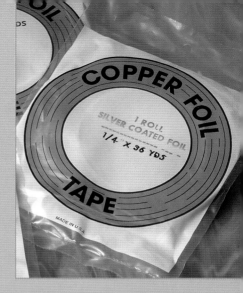

IF YOU HAVE BEEN WORKING WITH STAINED glass, you probably have most of the tools necessary to complete a lampshade. Depending on the projects you have completed thus far, a lot of the supplies might also be in your workshop.

The information discussed in this chapter lists and describes all of the items used in chapter 6 to build the featured shade. These items are also included on a checklist at the end of this chapter.

Working with Your Pattern

- **Tracing paper.** Translucent paper that allows lines from the original pattern to show through for tracing.
- **Carbon paper.** Inky blue or black paper that allows the design to be transferred onto the oak tag.
- **Oak tag.** Has a thickness similar to a manila file folder; used for assembling glass pieces prior to soldering.
- **Colored pencils.** Used to designate glass color on paper pattern pieces.
- **Rubber cement.** Used to attach paper pattern templates onto glass.
- **Scissors.** Used for cutting paper patterns and copper foil.
- **Pattern shears.** Special three-bladed shears that remove a thin strip of the paper pattern; reduces each pattern piece just enough so that when copper foil is applied to the pieces, the pattern returns to its original size.

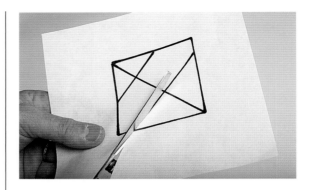

- **Glass markers.** Used primarily for writing numbers on glass—silver for dark glass and

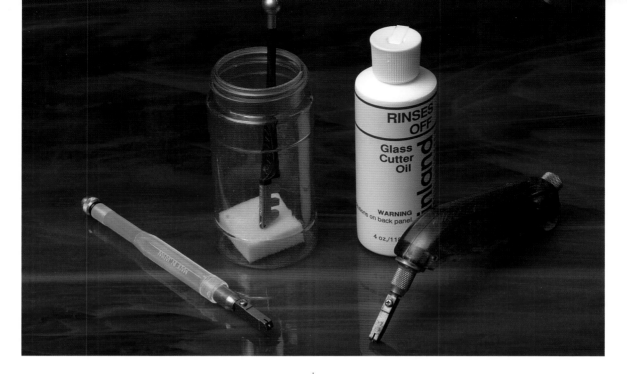

black for light glass. The marks will wash off with soap and water.

- **Homasote board.** Homasote makes a great work surface because it is removable, fire resistant, and soft enough for pins to be inserted, and it provides a slight cushion for cutting glass. Liquids will also bead up on it, so a spilled jar of flux is not a big problem. The Homasote board shown in chapter 6 is a 24-inch square.

Glass Cutters

- **Conventional glass cutter.** Available with a steel wheel or carbide wheel. (shown above in a jar with a sponge soaked in cutting oil).
- **Upright acrylic cutter (left)** Usually comes with a carbide wheel and is self-oiling.
- **Pistol cutter (right).** The pistol cutter's shape makes it comfortable to hold and allows you to use the larger muscles in your hand to apply pressure to the glass, resulting in less hand fatigue during extended cutting ses-

sions. These, too, are usually self-oiling.
- **Cutting oil.** Used to cool the cutting wheel. Reduces friction on the glass, resulting in more consistent cuts, and lubricates the wheel so it turns freely.

PRO TIP ✔

If you visit a local stained glass supply store, you have lots of choices in tools. Our experience over the years has made us firm believers that better tools, though costing more, are more effective in getting the job done and much more durable.

Whatever your approach, the three most important tools are the following:
- Glass cutter
- Breaking / Grozing pliers
- Soldering iron

If your resources are limited, buy the best of these tools that you can afford.

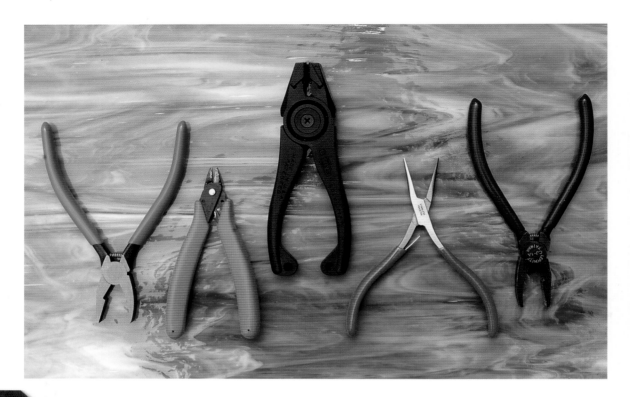

Pliers

- **Breaking/Grozing pliers.** Your main breaking tool; also used for grozing, as explained in chapter 3. Two types are shown on the far left and far right of the above picture. Also referred to as "combo" pliers.
- **Running pliers.** Used to separate glass along a score line. The upper jaw has a node on each side and the lower jaw has one in the middle (shown at left). When the pliers are centered on a score line, squeezing them causes the glass to "run" and separate.
- **Wire cutters (second from left).** Used for cutting the reinforcing wires on the lamp.
- **Needle-nose pliers (fourth from left).** Used to grip small pieces of glass and metal; can also be used to remove small glass shards during a repair job.

Copper Foil

Copper foil is the material that gets wrapped around each piece of glass prior to soldering. It is adhesive-backed, which makes for easy adherence. Because solder does not stick to glass, all glass edges must be covered with copper foil.

Copper foil is available in different thicknesses, widths, and color backings:

- Thicknesses range from .00100 mm to .00150 mm; we used .00125 mm, the most common thickness.

- Widths range from $1/8$ inch to $1/2$ inch. We used $7/32$-inch foil, which is probably the most common width.
- Copper foil can have a copper, black, or silver backing. If you are using a fairly transparent glass, the inside edges of the foil can be seen through the glass. If this is the case, use a foil that will match the patina you plan to use.

In our lamp, the band is transparent. We used black-backed foil because we planned to finish the shade with a black patina. Functionally, all foil works the same way; choosing a color backing is for aesthetics only.

Foiling Tools

The foiling instructions on pages 81 to 85 demonstrate how to apply foil by hand. Several foiling machines are also available.

- **Glass foiler.** The model shown here is mounted to a piece of wood, which is then attached to a work table with a quick-release clamp. The foiler comes with three sets of wheels to accommodate $3/16$-inch, $7/32$-inch, and $1/4$-inch foils. A guide in the foiler indicates where glass is inserted and centered. The glass is then rolled around a wheel, and the foil is attached. You will need only thirty minutes or so of practice on this tool to become proficient.
- **Fid.** Used for burnishing the foil to the glass.
- **Craft knife.** Used to trim or patch foil.

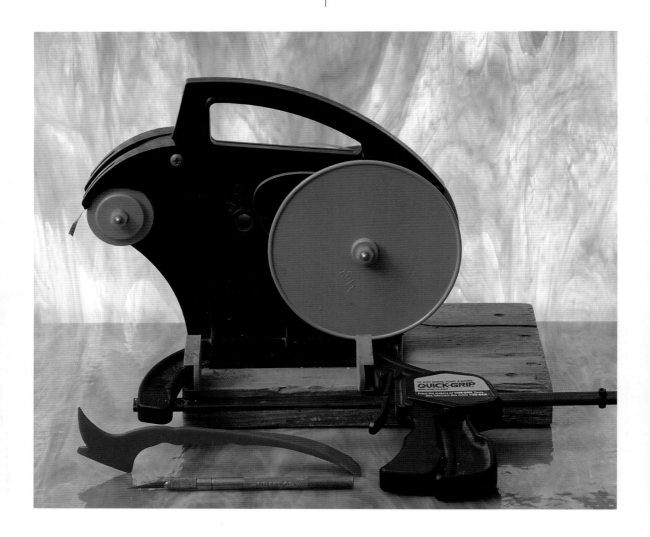

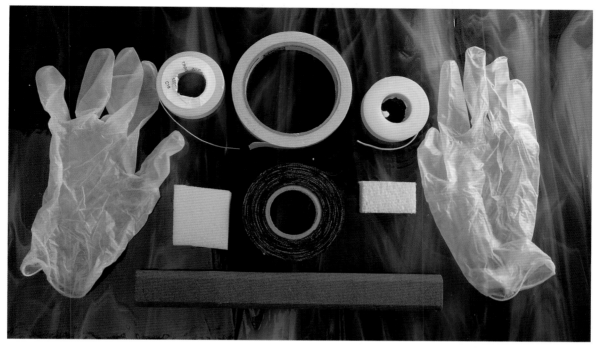

strips to be temporarily attached to your work board.

- **Lamp leveler.** Used to keep the lampshade level as you solder each seam.
- **Safety goggles.** Always wear comfortable, protective eyewear to avoid getting any glass chips in your eyes.
- **Rubber gloves.** Wear rubber gloves when applying patina to the lampshade.
- **Electrical tape.** Used to position and join the sections of the lampshade's cone prior to soldering.
- **Masking tape.** Temporarily prevents solder from melting through the holes in the lampshade as it is being built.
- **Carborundum stone.** Used to remove burrs and sharp edges from glass.
- **Cellulose sponges.** Used to remove debris and ash from soldering irons.
- **Inexpensive sponges.** Used to apply patina and then discarded.
- **Adhesive bandages and burn cream.**

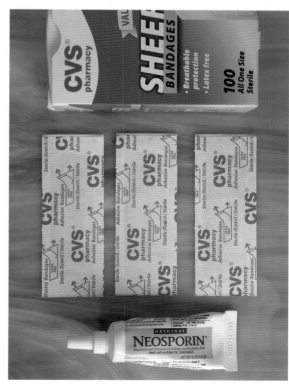

Wiring the Lamp

- **Lamp cap (vase cap).** Generally made of brass, the lamp cap gets soldered to the top of the shade. The small, diamond-shaped holes allow heat from the lightbulbs to escape.

- **Socket.** The fixture shown has three sockets so that light spreads evenly around the shade. The pull chains allow you to use one, two, or three bulbs at a time.
- **Chain.** Used to hang the shade from the ceiling.
- **Loop.** Screws on to the electrical fixture; the chain is attached to the upper part.

CHECKLIST: BUILDING A STAINED GLASS LAMPSHADE

Tools

- ☐ Soldering Iron
- ☐ Iron Stand
- ☐ Glass Cutter
- ☐ Breaking/Grozing Pliers
- ☐ Grinder
- ☐ Carborundum Stone
- ☐ Pattern Shears
- ☐ Glass Square
- ☐ Running Pliers
- ☐ Foiling Machine
- ☐ Foil Finisher
- ☐ Fids
- ☐ Craft Knife
- ☐ Utility Knife
- ☐ Needle-nose Pliers
- ☐ Wire Cutters
- ☐ Flux Brush

Chemicals

- ☐ Cutter Oil
- ☐ Flux
- ☐ Flux Remover
- ☐ Patina
- ☐ Finishing Compound
- ☐ Rubber Cement

Supplies

- ☐ 60/40 Solder
- ☐ $7/32$-inch Copper Foil
- ☐ Tracing Paper
- ☐ Carbon Paper
- ☐ Oak Tag
- ☐ Masking Tape
- ☐ Electrical Tape
- ☐ Soft Sponge
- ☐ Window Glass
- ☐ Assorted Glass
- ☐ Steel Wool
- ☐ 18-gauge Wire
- ☐ 3-bulb Socket Cluster
- ☐ Lamp Base

Miscellaneous

- ☐ Wood Blocks
- ☐ Scissors
- ☐ Layout Strips/Pushpins
- ☐ Cork-backed Ruler
- ☐ Colored Pencils
- ☐ Homasote Board
- ☐ Safety Glasses
- ☐ Markers
- ☐ Sponges
- ☐ Towels
- ☐ Bench Brush

Cutting Primer

A S YOU BEGIN THE TASK OF BUILDING A large stained glass lampshade, all of the steps are important and significantly affect subsequent steps. Glass cutting and soldering, however, are the two steps that require some extended practice. Knowing this, we have included detailed primers in these areas to get you prepared for the task at hand.

First of all, understand that the term glass cutting is a bit misleading. The glass cutter's wheel is rolled along a piece of glass, which produces a faint scratch—this is called scoring the glass. The glass has been weakened along this line and can now be broken in several ways. For the sake of clarity in this book, when the term glass cutting is used, it refers to the two-step process of scoring and breaking

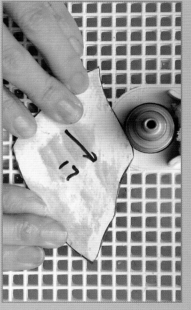

About Cutters

There are many different glass cutters on the market, most of which can be classified as either upright or pistol shaped. You should choose a cutter that is comfortable to use and easy to maneuver. If you plan to continue stained glass crafting beyond one lampshade, invest in a good cutter. There are numerous budget cutters on the market, but the old adage of getting what you pay for applies here. Our experience has shown that the better cutters work more effectively and last much longer. Plan to pay in the $30 to $45 range.

Holding the Cutter

Depending on the cutter you select, there are rather specific ways to hold it.

1 If you have the conventional metal cutter with a ball on top and notches in the back, make a V with the first two fingers of your dominant hand and slide the cutter between them. Place your index finger in the front grip slot and your thumb in the rear slot. This hand position allows you to steady the cutter.

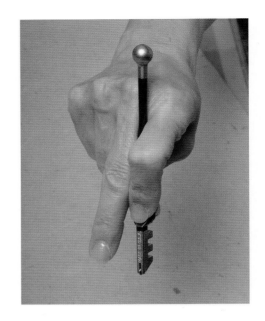

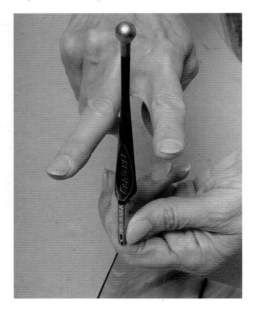

2 Place the thumb from your opposite hand on the ball or top of the cutter and your index finger along the side of the cutter.

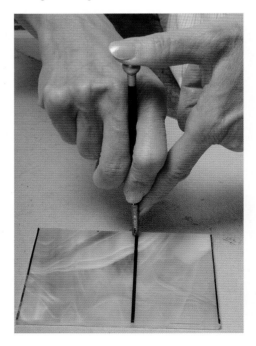

3 As you score, create pressure on the glass by pushing down with the thumb on the ball; your index finger helps you to guide the cutter. This cutter should be held perpendicular to the glass surface.

4 An effective grip for a cylindrical acrylic cutter is to hold it like a pencil in your dominant hand.

5 Now overlay this hand with your opposite hand, placing your index finger along the side of your cutter, just off the work surface. Your thumb rests on top of the hand holding the cutter.

PRO TIP ✔

Cutting oil is used to lubricate the cutting wheel. This keeps the wheel turning freely while reducing friction on the glass. For cutters without oil reservoirs, put a sponge in a baby food jar or other small container and saturate with oil. Dip your cutter in the oil every few times you make a score. You can also store your cutter in the jar when it is not in use.

6 Apply pressure from the three fingers holding the cutter in order to score the glass.

If you are using a pistol-shaped cutter, place it in your dominant hand with your thumb on top or off to one side.

7 Your opposite hand is overlapped on the first hand with your index finger along the side of the cutting wheel and just off the glass surface. The thumb from your opposite hand is placed so that it rests comfortably on your dominant hand. The cutter body should be parallel to the surface and the cutting head angled back about 20 degrees.

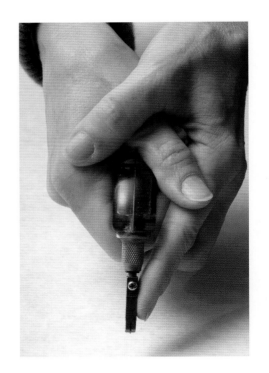

If you are holding the cutter as instructed, you are probably feeling a bit uncomfortable. Stick with it through the practice session—it will get easier.

For self-oiling cutters, add oil to approximately 10 percent of capacity. Overfilling leads to leakage, and a little oil lasts a long time. Each day you use your cutter, open the oil reservoir hole to allow air to enter. Failure to do this causes a vacuum to form, and oil may not feed onto the wheel.

Caution: When replacing the screw, tighten lightly so as not to force the screw into the plastic handle, which could split the seam. This will cause significant and continual leakage.

Cutting the Glass

As you begin the cutting practice, you should stand up. You will get better leverage on the cutter by using your shoulder and arm muscles, and you will be able to see better if you are directly over top of the work.

Now put your safety gasses on and get ready to cut glass.

1 On a sheet of glass approximately 4 x 8 inches, draw three lines across the 4-inch side: the first 1 inch from the edge, the second about midway, and the third 2 inches from the opposite end.

2 Place the cutting wheel on the middle line, about $1/16$ inch from the edge closest to you.

See the slot at the end of the cutter head? This is where the cutter's wheel is located. Starting now and lasting all through your entire stained glass career, train your eye to see this groove and line it up exactly with your pattern line each time you score glass.

3 Push the cutter down on the glass and move it along the pattern line until you reach about $1/16$ inch from the other end.

PRO TIP ✔

It's important to exert a proper pressure on the glass in order for it to break properly. A good score should produce a slight gritty noise and a very faint line.

In the photo at left, the score line on the far left is ideal. The other two have produced white powder and small fissures that are perpendicular to the score line. A good way to determine a proper pressure is to start with a light score (you should hear a little scratching). Use running pliers for safety and see if the glass separates accurately. If not, try scoring another line a bit deeper and so on until you achieve a successful pressure.

Caution: Never go over a score line twice. The score line will widen and become irregular, which makes breaking difficult. Double scoring can also damage your cutter.

4 Hold the glass tightly with your thumbs parallel to the score line and your index fingers bent and curled underneath. With a quick motion, roll your thumbs and hands outward, snapping the glass in two. The motion is similar to snapping a cracker in half.

Caution: Never try to break glass by rolling your thumbs inward. This can cause the glass to shatter.

5 Score the line that was drawn 1 inch from the edge. This time, break the glass with your breaking/grozing pliers (they will henceforth be referred to as combo pliers).

These pliers have a notched upper jaw and a curved lower jaw; both jaws are serrated. You can mark the upper jaw in order to locate it quickly.

6 Place your pliers perpendicular to the score line. The pliers should be close to the line, but not on or over it. Hold the pliers firmly and snap them down using the same outward movement as you did with the manual break. The back of your hand will bend down.

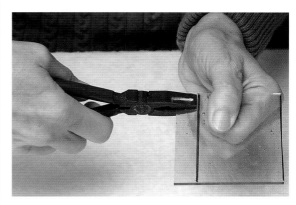

If you are seeing more marker line on one side of the glass, keep practicing to get your cutter in the center of the line.

7 Score the remaining line. Running pliers have a slight concave upper jaw with nodes on both sides—the upper jaw is marked in the middle. The lower jaw has a node in the middle. Place the pliers approximately $1/4$ inch onto the glass, lining up the indicator line on your pliers with your score line.

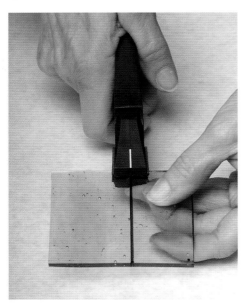

8 Gently squeeze the pliers together to separate the glass.

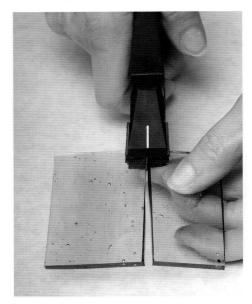

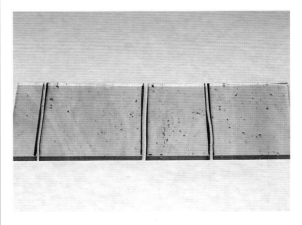

Cutting Basic Shapes

For the remainder of the cutting practice, you will need seven pieces of scrap or window glass about 4 by 4 inches and one piece about 5 by 7 inches.

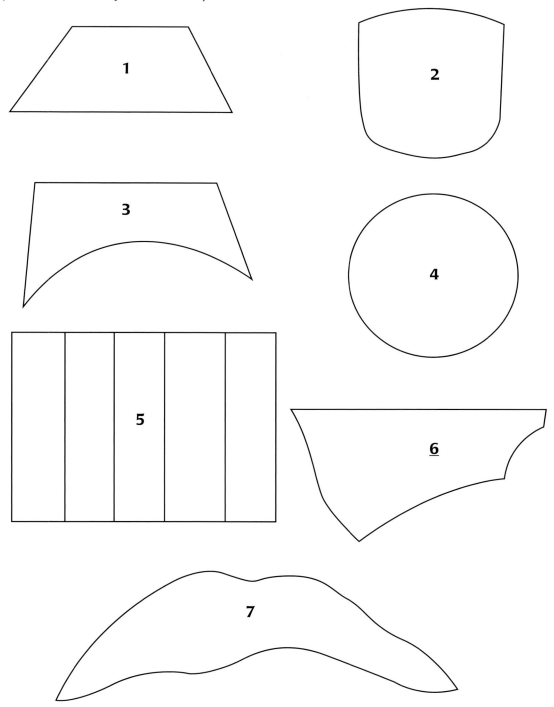

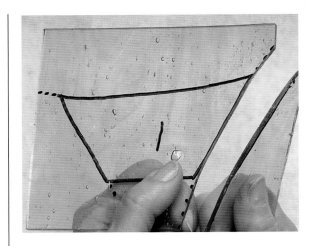

1   Draw the practice shapes 1, 2, 3, 4, 5, 6, and 7 on the smaller pieces of glass. Save the larger piece for later.

3   Score and break the remaining three sides using different breaking methods.

2   Starting with practice piece 1, begin on the edge closest to you and score along the line until you reach the opposite side. Remember to stop $1/16$ inch from the edge. Use a manual break to separate the glass.

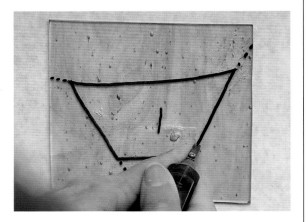

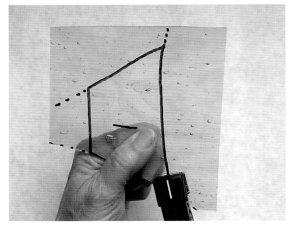

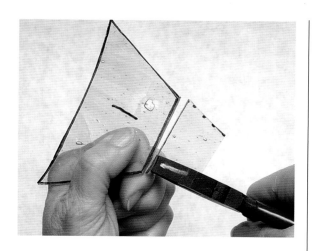

4   Although practice shape 2 has curved sides, you can cut it in the same fashion. Your combo pliers will work best on curves.

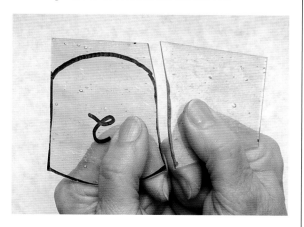

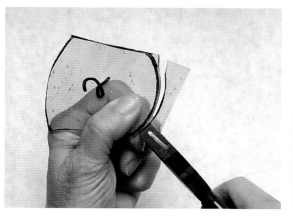

Cutting Inside Curves

Shape 3 represents the hardest pieces to cut—ones with inside curves. We drew two arcs and three partial arcs to show the sequence for cutting.

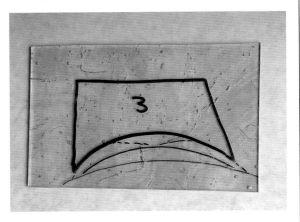

If the entire inside arc were scored at once, the glass would most likely break across the points at the bottom of the piece. Just because you score a piece and want it to break along the score doesn't mean that it will. A better strategy is to break out the curve in pieces.

1 Score and break the outermost arc, then do the same for the next arc.

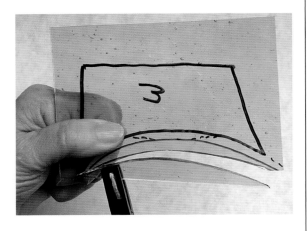

2 Score and break the small arc on the right or left, then score and break the opposite side arc.

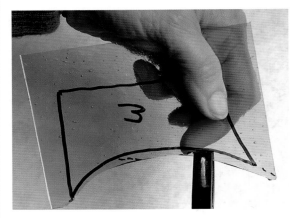

3 Score and remove the middle arc.

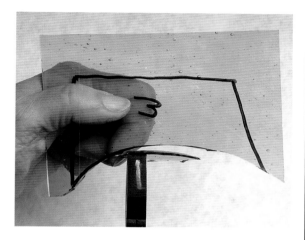

You have reduced the arc of a deep curve to a series of smaller, more manageable arcs.

4 Cut along the top of piece 3 and break manually or with running pliers.

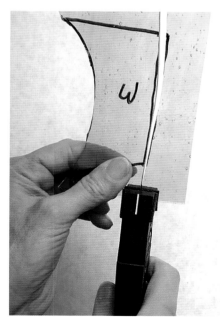

PRO TIP ✔

Avoid laying your pliers on a piece of glass you plan to use—this can chip or scratch your glass.

5 Cut the two remaining sides in either order. Score from the straight edges of the glass to each point, then break toward the point.

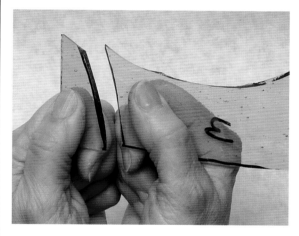

PRO TIP ✔

Although we had you draw the practice shapes on the glass, you will not use this technique for the lampshade design. Instead, you will learn how to attach paper patterns as templates.

Grozing

There may be several jagged spurs of glass still on your practice pieces. These need to be removed by grozing.

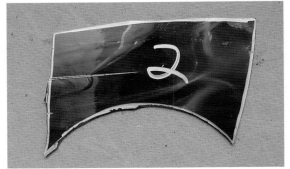

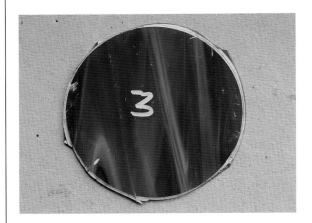

Grozing works best with the curved jaw of your pliers on top.

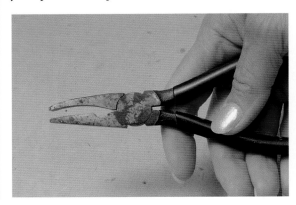

1 Turn your pliers so they are at about a 45-degree angle to the glass and put the jaws about $^1/16$ inch onto the glass where you intend to remove the excess.

2 Apply a firm grip to the pliers and rotate them down and away from the glass. *Note: remove only about $^1/16$ inch of glass at a time.* Holding the pliers at the same 45-degree angle, proceed along the area being removed. You are not trying to crush through the glass; rather, you are pulling away the small pieces.

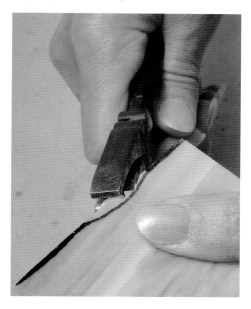

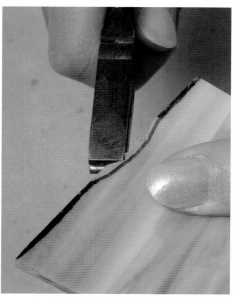

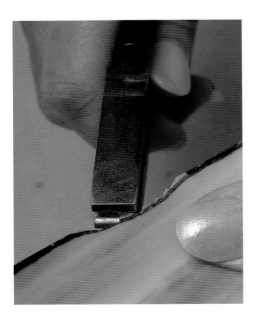

4 Continue grozing the rough edges on your remaining pattern pieces.

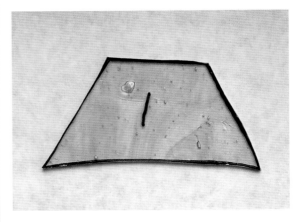

3 To remove the remaining rough edges, turn the pliers so they are perpendicular to the glass. Place them on the glass no more than $1/16$ inch, hold them firmly, and rotate them down and away. You may need to repeat these steps in the same area to get your desired result.

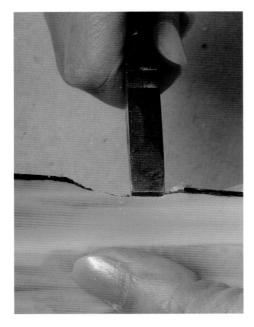

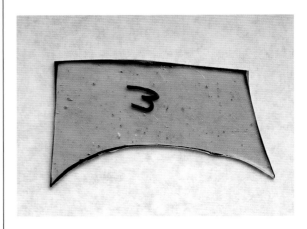

Cutting Circles

Circles consist of a series of outside curves. Although they still need to be cut in segments, outside curves will generally break away from the glass piece.

1   On practice piece 4, draw the dotted lines as shown.

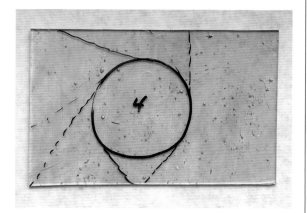

2   Starting with the arc on the bottom right side, score and break this section.

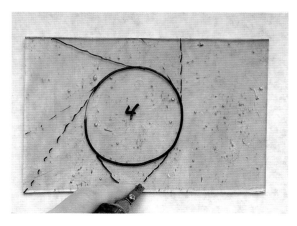

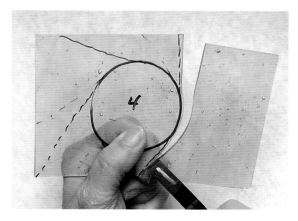

3   Continuing counterclockwise around the piece, cut the top right arc.

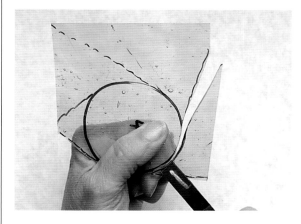

4 Cut the next arc.

5 Score and break the last segment; groze the circle as necessary.

It's almost impossible to break a perfect circle that doesn't need a bit of grozing.

Cutting Strips

Whether you are cutting strips of glass for borders around panels, box sides, or bands in lamps, it's important to learn how to cut them accurately. Because free-hand cutting may result in irregular edges, the use of a straight edge and a cutting square will be illustrated.

1 Place the 1-inch mark from your ruler on the bottom edge of practice piece 5. With your marker, place a dot at inches 2, 3, 4, 5, 6, and 7.

2 Place dots at every inch along the top as well.

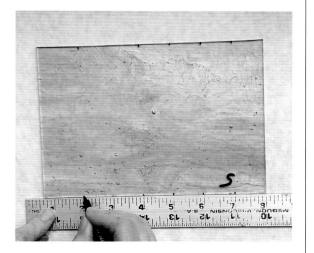

3 Line the wheel of your cutter against the ruler at the first bottom dot.

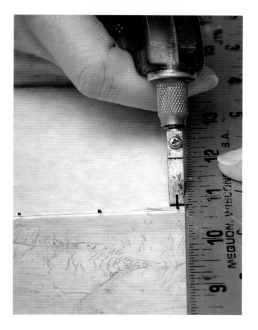

4 Repeat this for the first top dot, adjusting the ruler as needed.

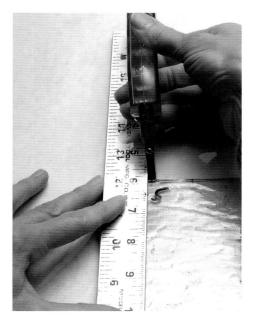

5 Holding the ruler securely in place, score the first strip, then break with running pliers.

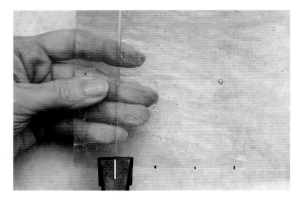

6 Cut the remaining strips in the same fashion.

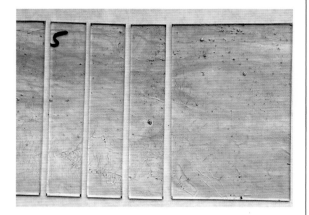

The real test comes when you put the strips together face to face. Are they even?

Try cutting another set of strips, this time using a cutting square.

1 Take another piece of glass about the same size and draw the dots in the same fashion.

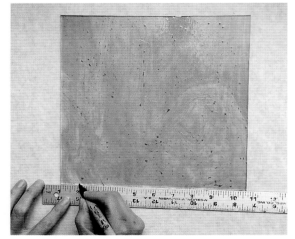

2 Place the cutting square on the bottom edge of the glass and line up the cutting wheel on the first dots, top and bottom.

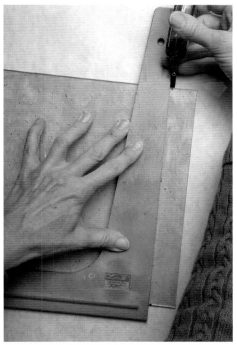

3 Score along the square and break with running pliers.

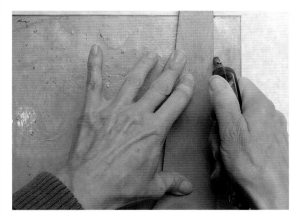

4 Cut the remaining strips.

Grinding the Glass

Once the glass has been cut and grozed, the final shaping can be done with either a carborundum stone or electric grinder.

1 If you are using a carborundum stone, wet it with water for about 10 seconds; this will keep the glass cool and dust to a minimum. On one of your practice pieces, firmly move the stone back and forth along the edge of the glass. Never use this stone perpendicular to the glass—it will chip the glass.

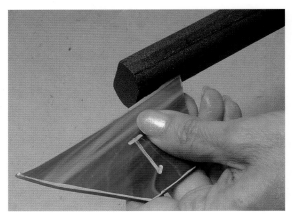

2 You can also rub the glass along a stationary stone to achieve the same results.

3 A more efficient method for smoothing lots of glass is to use an electric grinder. This specialty tool employs a water-cooled diamond grinding drum. Glass grinders are safe, fast, and effective.

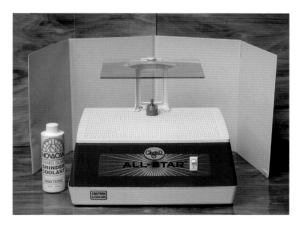

A small sponge is soaked in water then placed behind the grinder wheel to keep the glass cool as grinding occurs. Lay the glass flat on the grinder surface.

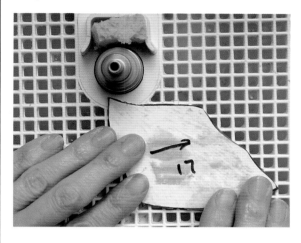

3 Using moderate pressure, push the glass against the wheel. As the excess glass is eliminated, slowly move the glass along the wheel.

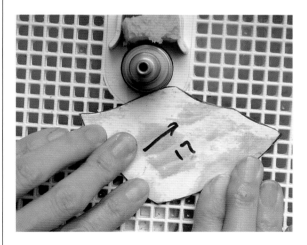

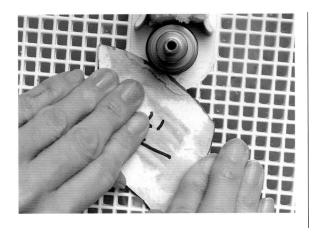

A perfectly ground piece is one that shows no glass protruding beyond the paper pattern.

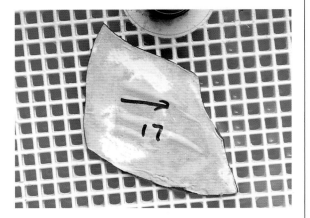

PRO TIP ✔

When using a grinder, push the glass in one direction and avoid a back-and-forth sawing motion. If you notice a buildup of dry powder when you are grinding, rinse your sponge and add more water to the grinder. Make sure the sponge is making contact with the grinding drum.

More Practice

Practice shapes 6 and 7 are found in the featured lampshade pattern.

1 Start with the large inside curve on piece 6.

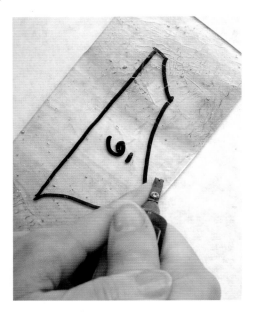

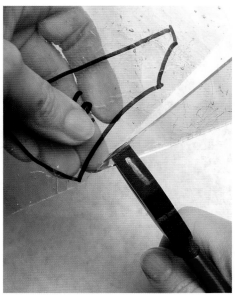

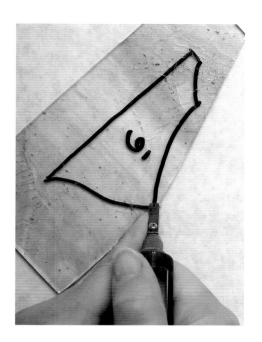

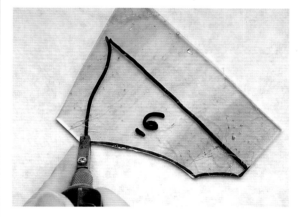

2 Cut the other sides in the order shown below.

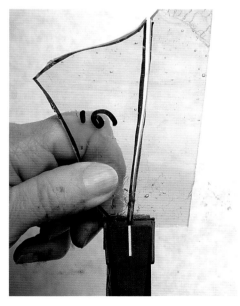

3 Piece 7 is the most challenging piece in the lamp pattern. Cut the inside curve first.

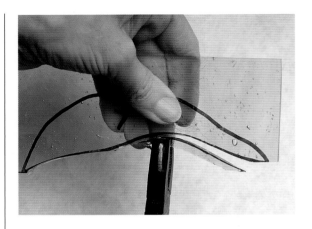

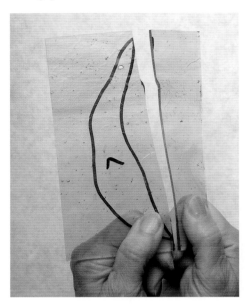

4 Then cut the outside curve.

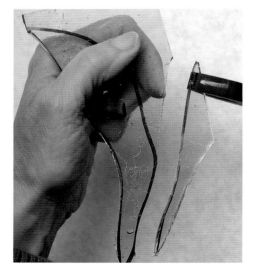

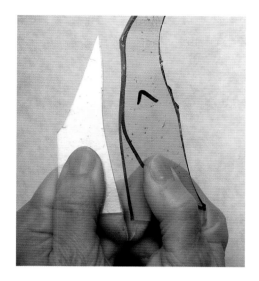

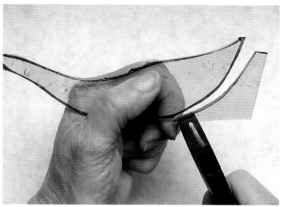

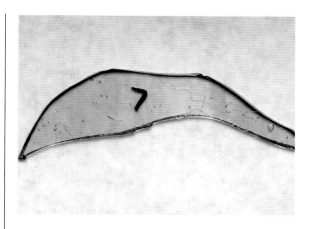

This concludes the cutting practice primer. If you are not feeling confident with your cutting, repeat some of the practice pieces. After the chapter on soldering, we have included an optional panel for you to build so you can gain some experience with soldering as well as additional cutting.

5 Groze as necessary.

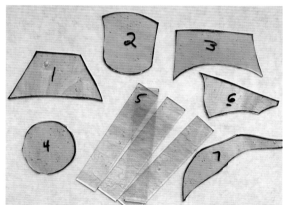

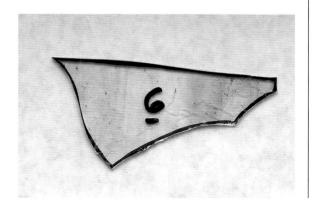

4

Soldering Primer

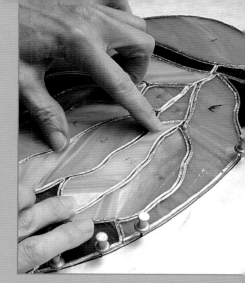

OVER THE PAST TWO DECADES, WE'VE HAD more than three thousand students come through our studio doors. Nearly everyone has come in feeling that cutting would be the most difficult part of stained glass crafting. After about an hour or so on the first day of class, however, most people realize that cutting is not too bad. And after our initial seven-and-a-half-hour course, they feel pretty good about their cutting ability.

Soldering is a different story. The majority of our new students struggle to achieve consistently smooth solder seams. Smooth seams will come eventually, but they take some time.

If you have not done much or any soldering, it is highly recommended that you practice on a flat panel before you start building your lamp. Making the "Waiting for Fall" oval panel, which we illustrate here, will provide you with considerable soldering practice. It could also dress up a small kitchen window or serve as a nice gift for Mother's Day. Build it with or without the outside glass border.

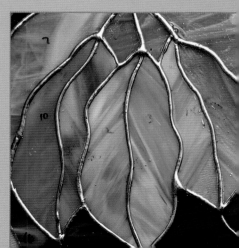

45

Getting the Project Ready

Before beginning this project, you might want to look at the opening steps in chapter 6 to learn how to set up the pattern, use pattern shears to cut apart the pattern, attach paper patterns to the glass, cut and grind the glass, and foil the glass pieces.

1 Enlarge two copies of the pattern to the recommended size, or make it smaller or larger, as desired. Number and color-code the pieces, and include directional arrows.

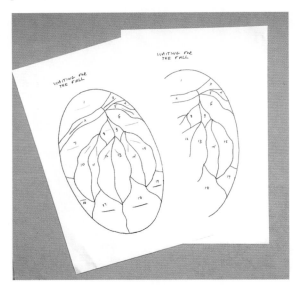

2 Use pattern shears to cut apart the pattern; pattern shears will ensure that there is space between the pieces for the copper foil.

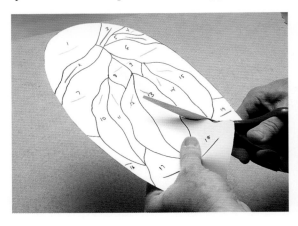

3 Affix pattern pieces to the glass with rubber cement.

4 Cut, groze, and grind the glass pieces.

5 Wash the glass pieces.

6 Wrap each piece in $^3/_{16}$- or $^7/_{32}$-inch copper foil

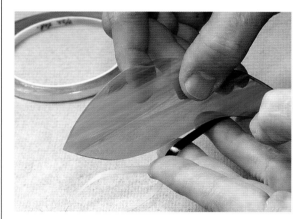

Securing the Project to the Work Surface

1 Arrange all the foiled glass pieces on a copy of the pattern.

2 Because the design is oval, the layout bars shown in chapter 6 will not be used to secure the pieces in place. Instead, you can space pushpins around the perimeter of the oval. Place the pushpins right up against the pieces of glass.

3 Apply flux to all the copper foil seams. One brushful of flux should be enough to cover the entire panel. Do not put flux on the outside edges.

4 Adjust any pieces of the project that might have moved during the flux application.

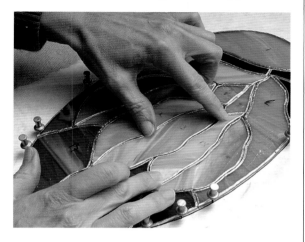

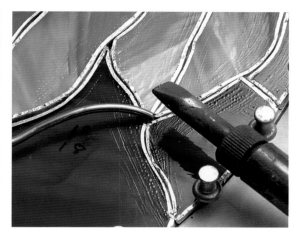

5 As your iron heats up, ash may form on its tip. Clean this off by rubbing the iron on a wet sponge. Rub both sides once.

6 As you begin to solder, you will discover that the pushpins keeping the glass pieces from moving are in your way. The first step is to tack-solder the pieces together so the pushpins can be removed.

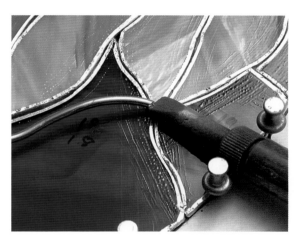

7 Unravel about 6 inches of solder from the spool. Your iron should be held in your dominant hand and the solder in the other. Put the solder on an intersection where three pieces of glass touch. Use the flat part of the iron tip to melt off a $1/8$-inch segment of solder. The iron should rest on the copper as the solder melts. When the solder has melted, lift the solder out of the way and then lift the iron. Each tack should take 2 to 3 seconds.

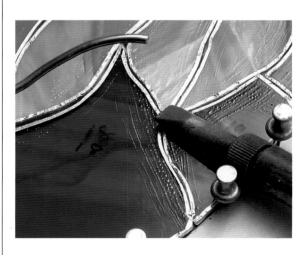

Remember: Melt the solder, lift the solder, and then lift the iron.

8 Tack-solder all intersections.

9 Remove the pushpins and pull out the paper pattern.

PRO TIP ✔

When you first heat up your iron, you should clean your iron tip. The iron is subjected to very high temperatures (700-plus degrees), and ash frequently gets baked onto the tip. This impedes the transfer of heat, preventing the solder from melting.

Sal ammoniac is a chemical block that loosens the ash.

1 Dig out a small trough on a sal ammoniac block and melt a small amount of solder in it.

2 Rub both sides of the iron back and forth in the molten solder. Clean the tip in the sponge and resume soldering.

When you solder for an extended period, you might sense the iron cooling down—it probably just needs to be cleaned in the sal ammoniac bar.

10 The iron should be held parallel to the glass, so hold it as if you are shaking hands or holding a sword. Tilt the iron to approximately a 45-degree angle and let it rest on the copper seam.

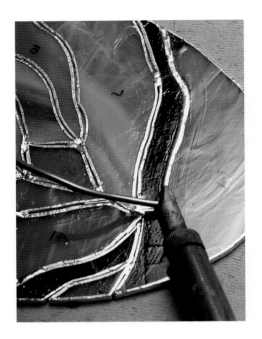

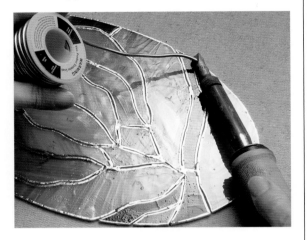

11 Starting at any seam toward the top of the panel, find a hot spot on the iron where the solder melts rapidly. Push solder to it and begin pulling the iron toward you, allowing the solder to flow down the iron tip onto the copper seam.

12 For this initial phase of soldering, don't worry about how it looks; just apply a rather flat coating to the entire panel.

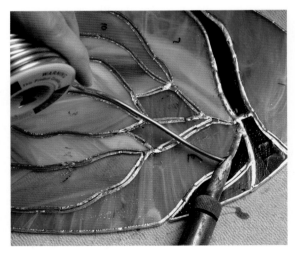

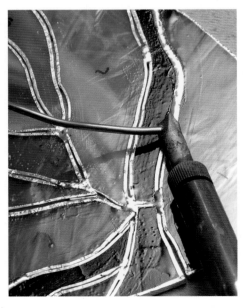

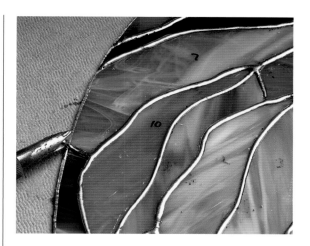

If you add a small amount of flux prior to adding the second (beaded) coating of solder, the solder will flow better. As soon as solder cools, it can begin to oxidize; flux will clean this off.

13 The beaded coat is applied in the same fashion as the initial coating. Add additional solder and slowly pull the iron toward you as the solder melts. The overall result should be a smooth and rounded mound of solder that is consistent in height across the entire panel.

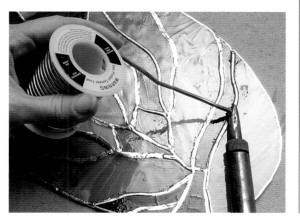

Several variables will affect your ability to produce a smooth, consistent solder bead:

- **Heat of the iron.** 700 to 800 degrees is where you want to be with most irons. To test the temperature of the iron, melt a small amount of solder on its tip. If it melts instantly and stays on the tip, the temperature is about right. If it takes a second or more to melt, increase the temperature. If the solder falls off your tip, it is too hot—cool it down.

- **Speed at which you move the iron.** If you move too slow, solder will melt through the project to the opposite side, as shown at right.

  If you move too fast, the solder flow will not be consistent, and you will end up with high and low spots on the solder seams.

- **Invest in a quality soldering iron.** Purchase either an iron with a temperature control device built in or a more basic iron and a separate temperature controller. Expect to pay between $40 and $100. Always use a quality liquid or gel flux and 60/40 solder.

14 When you are satisfied with the first side, turn over the panel and apply flux to the other side.

15 Position the iron as before and begin melting solder on the seams. Because you have gained some experience from soldering the first side and you are using less solder, the opposite side's solder should go on a lot easier.

PRO TIP: SOLDER PROBLEMS AND SOLUTIONS ✔

Solder will often flow from one side to the other and leave a puddle blemish, as shown.

There are three ways to deal with this depending on the quantity of solder:

1   If it is only a small amount, flux the area and smooth it out with your iron.

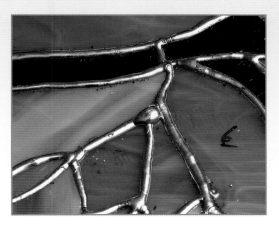

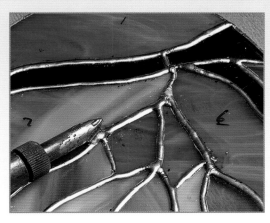

2 If you need to remove a larger amount, melt a small area and gently flick it onto the glass. Do this several times until the area is rounded again.

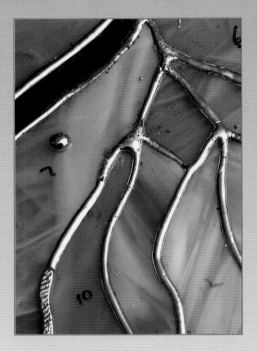

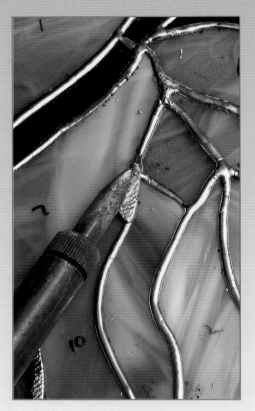

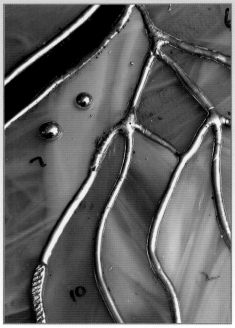

PRO TIP: SOLDER PROBLEMS AND SOLUTIONS ✔

3 Hold your iron parallel to the glass. Melt off a small amount of solder from the blemish (a little less than the width of your iron tip) and lift the iron slightly. The solder should adhere to the iron, and you can then deposit it onto your work surface. If the solder does not adhere to the iron, the iron is too hot, so you must cool it down in your wet sponge.

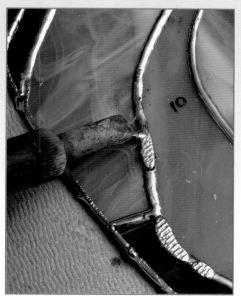

PRO TIP: SOLDER PROBLEMS AND SOLUTIONS ✔

4 If bubbles or divots form on the solder seams, touch the iron to the area and allow it to melt for 1 to 2 seconds. Then lift your iron straight up.

5 If blobs of solder harden on the outside edge of the panel, move the panel to the edge of the work surface, melt the solder, and allow it to drop onto the table. If you are concerned about burning your table, drop the solder onto a piece of cardboard.

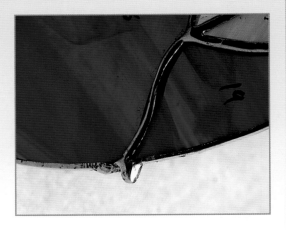

16 Return to the front side to see if any solder melted through. If it did, either smooth it out or remove it.

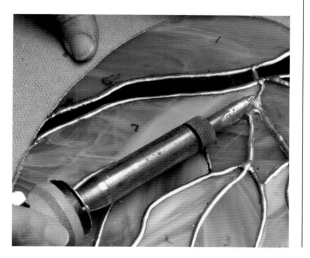

Soldering is arguably the most difficult step to master, but it does get easier the more you do. If you need help in finishing the oval, all the details will be explained in chapter 6. For help with attaching the lead came on the outside, see *Basic Stained Glass Making* (Stackpole Books, 2003).

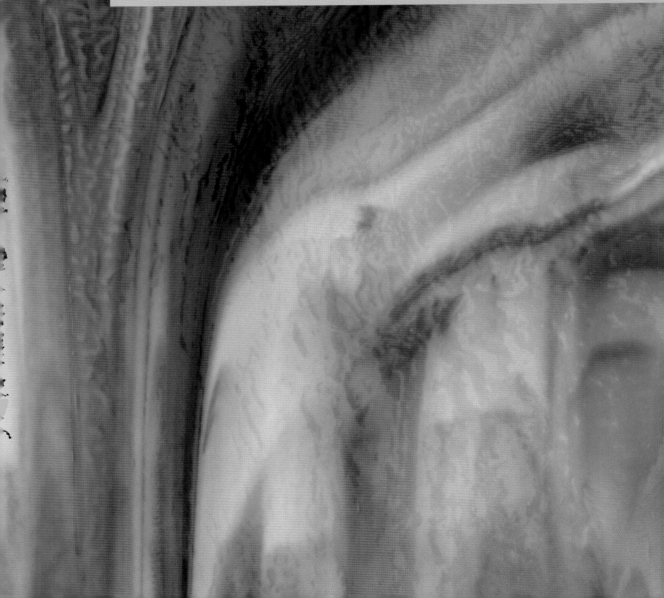

5

Selecting Your Glass

IF YOU EVER HAVE AN OPPORTUNITY TO VISIT a Tiffany lamp exhibit, take a good look at the glass that was used. Note the prevalence of multicolored glasses, the color striations, shadings, translucency and textures, and how many of the organic shapes of leaves and flower petals are so well represented by specific pieces of glass. These are some of the subtle features that make the nicer Tiffany shades stand out.

So how do you go about making your lampshade truly spectacular? In the Tiffany tradition, you should start with the selection of your glass.

Types of Glass

There are literally thousands of different colors and styles of stained glass manufactured today.

Cathedral

Cathedral glasses are transparent in nature and available in many different textures that alter the degree of transparency.

Smooth Cathedral

Hammered

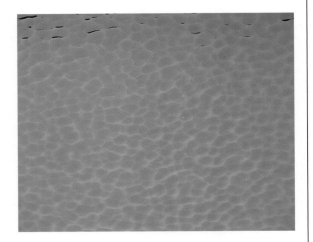

Granite

Seedy

Glue Chip

Ripple. This Wissmach glass was used for the band of our featured lamp.

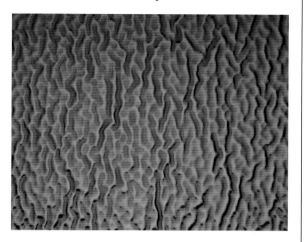

Water Glass

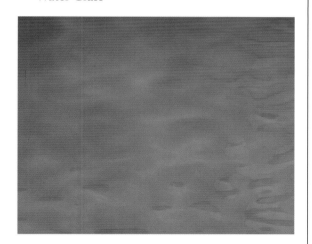

Streaky

Streaky glasses are cathedrals with one or more other colors. They may be smooth or textured like granite, ripple, or water glass.

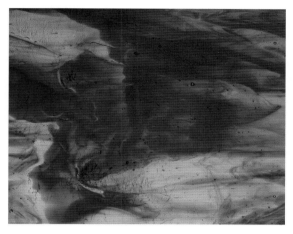

Opalescent

Opalescent glasses, also known as opals, are made up of varying amounts of white (opal) glass mixed with colored glass. The higher the opal content, the denser the glass will be. Some opals are one solid color, but most have two or more colors.

Iridescent opals have a metallic surface on the top.

Wispy opals transmit the most light because almost three quarters of the glass is cathedral.

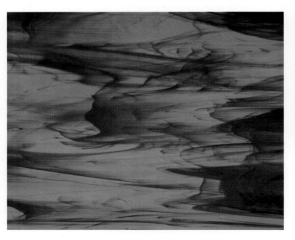

Translucent opals have almost the same amounts of opal and cathedral, reducing light transmission. This Spectrum glass was used as the background in our featured lamp.

This Kokomo glass was used as one of the leaf colors in our featured lamp. Note the variety of color striations that offer lots of subtle options within the same piece of glass.

A new innovative surface available from Spectrum Glass Company is their Corsica texture, which resembles a soft granite finish. It can be found in their entire line of "Pearl Opal" glasses. When light is transmitted through the glass, the result is a very interesting sparkle.

The white glass in the cone and background of the fall color version of our featured lamp is Spectrum Pearl Opal (60008).

Youghiogheny Stipple is a specialty opal glass with a waxlike transparency. The leaves in the photo below are all stipple glasses.

Assorted hand-rolled art glasses

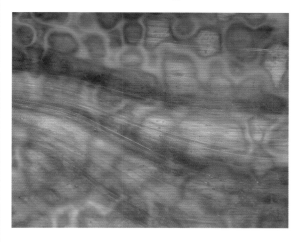

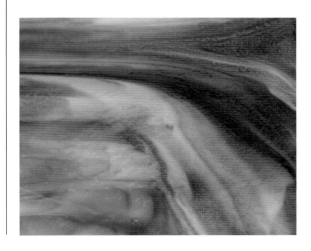

Bevels, Jewels, and Nuggets

Bevels are precut pieces of clear glass with angled edges that create a prism or rainbow effect when sunlight passes through them. They are available in a multitude of sizes and shapes.

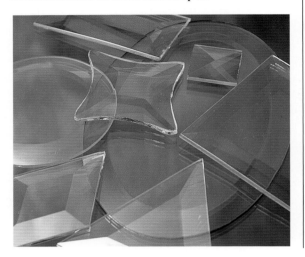

Jewels are pieces of glass that resemble precious stones. They are available in many colors and shapes and can be faceted or smooth.

Nuggets, also known as globs, are irregularly shaped pieces of glass.

Choosing Glass for Your Lampshade

When you visit a stained glass supply store for the first time, you might be a bit overwhelmed by all the glass choices. Here are a few things to consider when selecting glass:

- By using translucent glass, you will maximize the amount of light and color. A dense glass will block light from passing through. A streaky or cathedral glass might create too much glare from the bulbs or reveal the light fixture.
- What colors do you want to feature? A helpful exercise is to view pictures of lamps created by professional craftsmen in stained glass design books. These will illustrate a variety of color combinations.

- This is your lamp, and you are allowed to express yourself. Nothing anywhere says that leaves have to be green or red or orange. Browns work, as do blues and purples.
- Some glasses are kind of boring; others are very vibrant and exciting. The right glass will bring the lamp to life.
- When selecting glass, make sure you see how it looks when backlit by incandescent light. Does it light up the way you want it to?
- Make sure you buy enough glass. Some areas on a sheet of glass cannot be used because of blemishes, too little or too much color, transparency, and so on. Particularly if you are using art glass, you will need a little extra.

What We Used

The following glass selections were used in our featured lamp, its color alternative, and the alternative design.

Featured Leaves

- Cone—Spectrum 3471 (pale purple/white translucent)
- Band—Wissmach 134 Rip (medium rose ripple)
- Leaves—Kokomo 48 (medium green)
  Kokomo 122 (two greens opal)
  Kokomo 86 (dark green/white opal)

Alternate Leaves

- Cone—Spectrum 600081 (pearl/white pearl opal)
- Band—Wissmach 48 Rip (medium Amber ripple)
- Leaves—Youghiogheny 1109sp (red stipple)
  Youghiogheny 1097sp (red/green stipple)
  Youghiogheny 5409sp (yellow/orange stipple)

"Graceful Flowers"

- Cone—Spectrum 603383 (blue/white pearl/opal)
- Band—Armstrong 105 (black/gray streaky)
- Flowers—Wissmach 145sp (honey wispy opal) and Wissmach 11LL (red/amber streaky)
- Leaves—Kokomo 48G (medium green granite) and Kokomo 86G (dark green granite)

Quantity of Glass Needed

- Background—5 square feet
- Leaves—3 square feet (1 square foot of each color)
- Band—1 square foot

6

Building a Stained Glass Lampshade

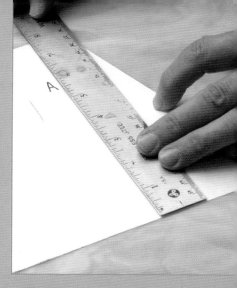

ALL THE INFORMATION FROM THE PRECEDING chapters will help you construct a beautiful stained glass lampshade. As you begin, read all the directions and refer to the basic skills sections if necessary. And be patient! Some crafters will finish the lamp in a weekend. Most will take between a week and a month. A few will take even longer. Speed is not an issue here—take your time and build it well.

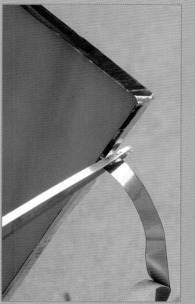

Parts of a Lampshade

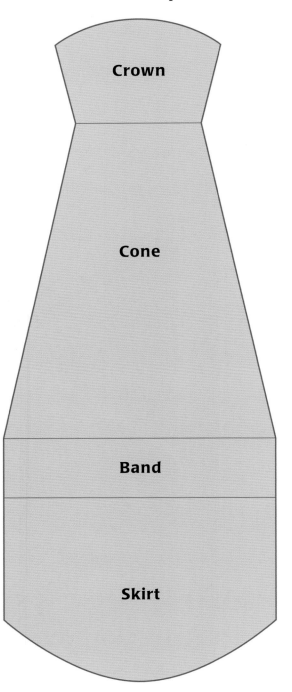

Crown

Cone

Band

Skirt

Preparing the Patterns

You will need to make multiple working copies of your lamp design. First make nine copies of the upper, or cone, section. Eight will be for cutting your glass pieces and one will be for laying out the glass pieces prior to soldering.

Then make five copies each of the band and skirt designs A/B and C/D (four for cutting and one for the layout).

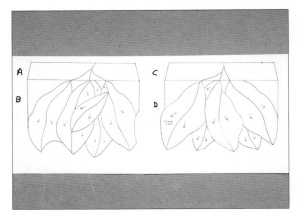

Each of the eight cone sections is made up of only two pieces of glass, but it is important to make sure that the glass pieces from each section stay matched together through the soldering stage.

PRO TIP ✔

Always make an extra copy of any design you are using for your "pattern file." You might just get a request to build a custom-colored shade for a family member or friend and earn a few dollars in the process.

1 To do this, mark an A on both pieces of the first cone section.

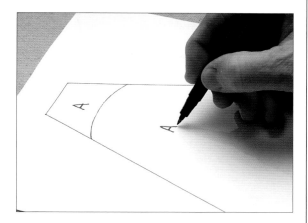

2 Mark the remaining sections B through H in the same fashion.

3 It is very important, from an aesthetic standpoint, that the color graining on each of the cone sections is running in the same direction. Decide whether you want the color graining to run around (horizontally) or up and down (vertically). Neither is necessarily right or wrong—it is simply your preference.

4 Indicate your preference by drawing a line on both pieces of each cone section. Notice that we used a purple colored pencil for the small top pieces of the cone and orange for the larger pieces. These same colors will be used again when we prepare the skirt sections of the shade.

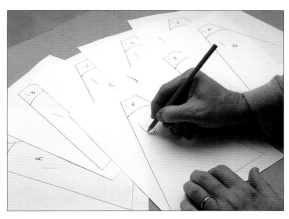

5 Use regular scissors to cut along the outside lines of each pattern sheet.

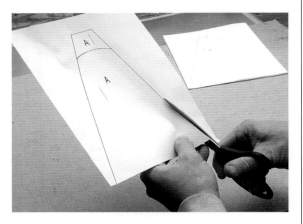

6 Then use pattern shears to cut down the middle of the arch that separates the two pieces of each section.

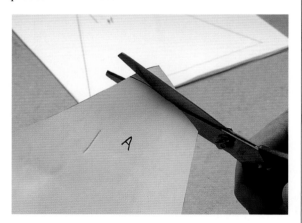

Cutting the Glass

Now that the patterns have been cut apart and organized, you are ready to cut the glass for the cone sections. To cut the larger pieces of the cone, start with a piece of glass that is at least 24 inches wide—this will help minimize glass waste. If you use commonly available 12-by-12-inch pieces of glass, you will need eight squares and will have considerable waste.

1 Measure the height of the pattern piece—it should be approximately $7^3/4$ inches.

2 Measure 8 inches along the bottom edge of the glass sheet and make a mark. Remember to keep the direction of your color grain in mind.

3 Measure 8 inches along the top edge of the glass and make a mark.

4 Using a ruler that is at least as long as the width of the glass, line up your cutter on both marks and adjust the ruler against the cutter.

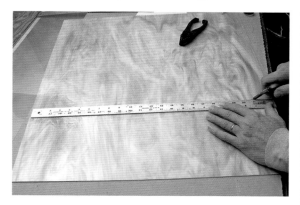

5 Score along the ruler, then separate the glass with your running pliers.

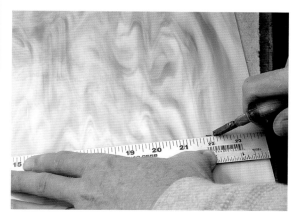

6 Repeat steps 2 through 5 to cut another strip of glass. Two strips at least 24 inches wide each will yield the eight pieces needed for your lamp.

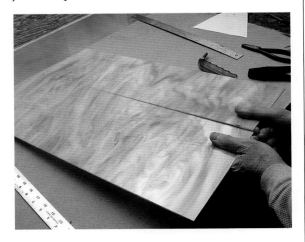

7 Use rubber cement to attach the larger pattern pieces, A–H, to the glass. The base of pattern piece A should be flush with the bottom edge of the glass strip.

8 Pattern piece B should be reversed so that its base is flush with the top edge of the glass. Separate A and B by approximately $1/2$ inch so the breaks will be clean, eliminating rough edges.

9 Attach pattern pieces C and D in the same sequence.

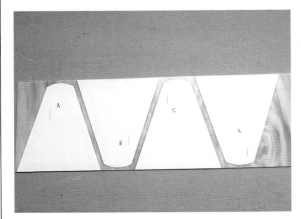

10 Attach pattern pieces E–H on the second strip of glass in the same fashion.

The glass for the smaller pieces of the cone is prepared in the same way.

1 Measure the height of the pattern piece. It should be approximately $1^1/2$ inches. Add an additional $^1/4$ inch to avoid breaking the points, making the total height $1^3/4$ inches.

2 Cut strips $1^3/4$ inches wide, allowing for the grain direction you have chosen.

3 Measure $1^3/4$ inches along the bottom of the glass and mark.

4 Measure $1^3/4$ inches along the top of the glass and mark.

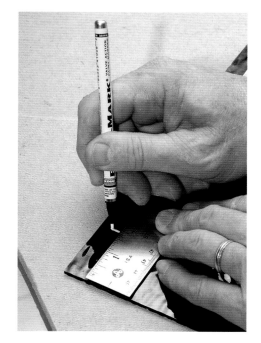

5 Line up your ruler on the marks and cut the strip.

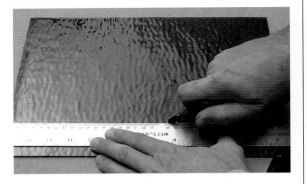

6 Cut a second strip the same width, then attach the pattern pieces to the glass. Because we used a heavy textured glass (ripple) and wanted the texture to be on the outside, we turned the pattern pieces upside down and attached them to the smooth side of the glass. *Remember:* Always cut on the smoother side of the glass.

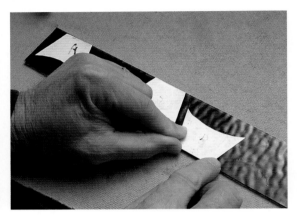

PRO TIP ✔

When using textured glass, you may choose either side to face out. Neither is right or wrong. The decision is based purely on aesthetics—which look do you prefer? I generally use the texture on the outside, but you may do otherwise.

7 Starting with the large glass strips, use your ruler to score the long side of piece A adjacent to piece B. Position the ruler so the wheel of the cutter rolls along the glass, flush up against the paper pattern.

8 Score and break the other long side of piece A, again making sure the cutter wheel is flush against the paper pattern.

9 Score the remaining glass on piece A, then break it off with breaking pliers.

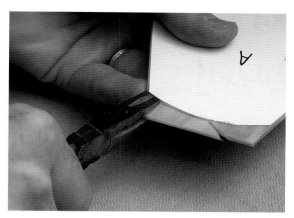

10 Cut the remaining pieces B–H in the same way.

11 As you begin to cut apart the small pieces of each cone section, remember to cut the inside curve first. The curve is not deep enough to warrant several cuts, but it will be helpful to cut the curve with at least two scores.

12 Score around the curve, leaving about $1/4$ inch of glass attached. Break off the scored piece.

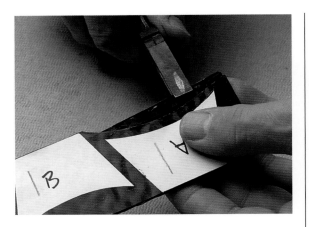

13
Score and break the remaining glass in the curve.

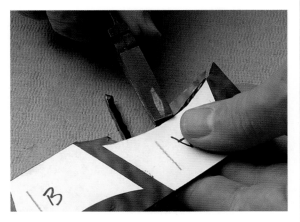

14
Cut the remaining sides of small piece A.

15
Repeat these cutting steps for small pieces B–H.

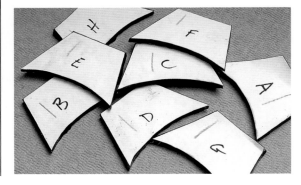

Grinding and Washing

Assuming that the straight edges of the glass pieces do not need any grinding, you can work on the outside curves of the large pieces and the inside curves of the small pieces. If any of the straight edges of the pieces have excess glass, you can grind these edges as well.

1 Remember to grind right up to the paper pattern.

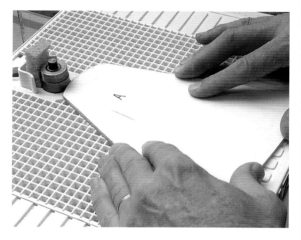

2 As you complete both parts to section A, put them together to see that they fit. If any glass protrudes from either side of the curve, and the pieces do not fit evenly, grind as necessary. Repeat for sections B through H.

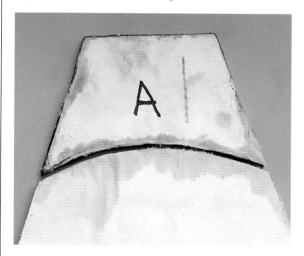

3 When all sections are fitted to your liking, peel off the paper patterns and mark each piece of glass with its letter code.

The glass must be squeaky clean in order for the copper foil to adhere properly. Prepare a basin of detergent and water and another basin with warm water.

1 Submerge both A pieces in the detergent. Clean the outside edges and the top and bottom surfaces with a sponge.

2 Rinse the pieces in the warm water basin.

3 Carefully dry the pieces with a clean towel.

4 If the letter mark washes off, reapply it.

Foiling the Glass Pieces

Copper foil is synonymous with the "Tiffany method" by which stained glass is joined together to form windows and lamps. The process dates back to the second half of the 1800s and is often attributed to Louis Comfort Tiffany. Copper foil is adhesive-backed and comes in an array of sizes and color backings. We used $7/32$-inch foil, which is considered to be medium-sized, to accommodate the larger pieces in the cone of our lampshade.

1 Begin by peeling 2 or 3 inches of backing from the foil.

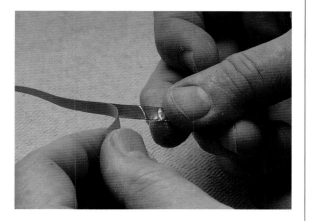

2 Place the foil between your index and middle fingers with the foil facing you.

3 Center the foil on a flat edge of the glass several inches from either end. By looking over both sides of the glass, you will see how centered the glass appears. You do not have to measure the foil; if it looks even on both sides, that will be close enough.

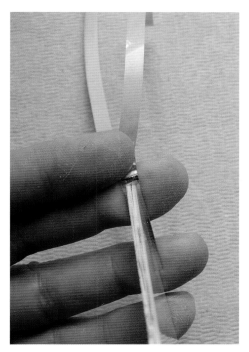

4 Press the foil to the glass so that it adheres.

5 Begin rolling the glass forward onto new foil, keeping the glass centered.

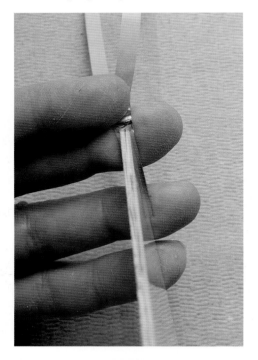

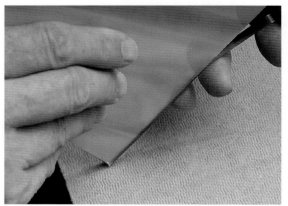

6 Continue applying the foil all the way around the glass piece.

7 When you come to your original starting point, overlap the foil about $1/4$ inch, then cut it with scissors.

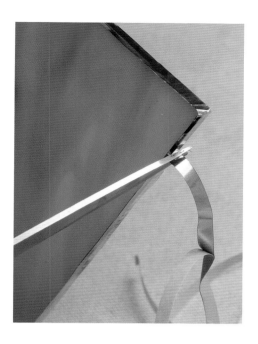

9 Use your fingernail to fold down the top left flap of the foil.

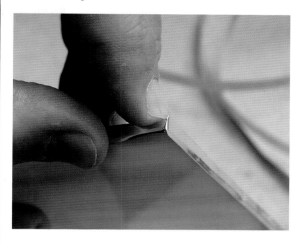

8 Press the foil to the glass all around the piece so that it is well adhered, but don't fold it over yet.

10 Fold down the remaining three flaps, one at a time.

11 With your thumb and index finger, fold the foil along a straight edge. As you get to a new corner, fold the foil as you did at the first corner.

12 Finish folding down the foil on the rest of the piece.

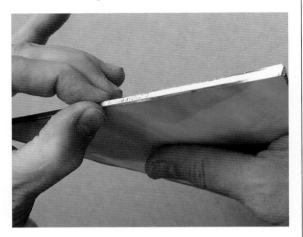

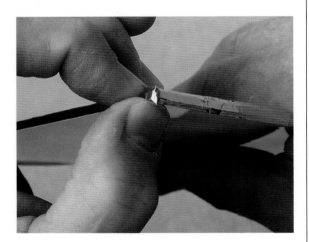

After the foil has been folded down around the entire piece, it needs to be burnished to the glass for proper adhesion.

1 Hold the foil finisher perpendicular to one edge of the glass. Push the foil finisher over the glass so the glass passes between the two rollers.

2 Continue pushing the finisher around the glass until all the foil is burnished. As you can see, both the top and bottom edges are burnished in one pass.

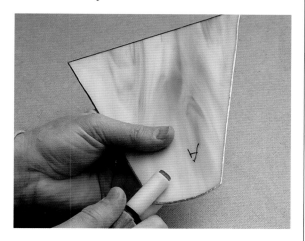

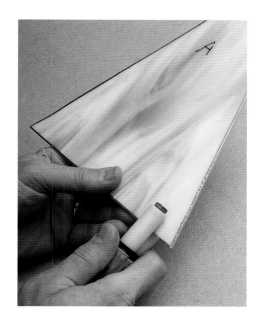

You can also burnish the foil by using a fid instead of a foil finisher.

1 Using the wide flat surface on a fid, apply pressure to the top edge of the glass, and continue around the perimeter of the glass. Turn the glass over and repeat on the bottom edge.

2 Foil all sixteen pieces that make up the lamp's large cone.

Forming the Lampshade's Cone

The first step in building the lampshade's cone is to solder together the two pieces of glass that form each of the eight cone sections. Time to plug in your soldering iron!

1 Attach a layout strip along the top line of the pattern using pushpins.

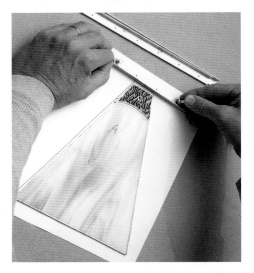

2 Attach a second strip along the left side.

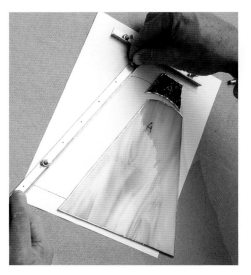

3 Place the two A glass pieces against the strips, then attach the right layout strip.

4 Attach a fourth strip along the bottom line of the pattern. The strips will hold the pieces in place while you solder them together.

5 Apply flux to the seam between the two pieces.

6 Tack-solder the pieces on the right and left sides.

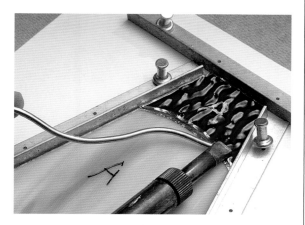

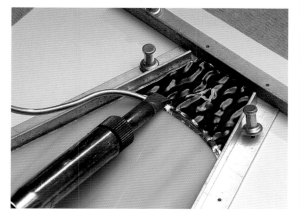

7 Remove the bottom layout strips and lift out the glass section.

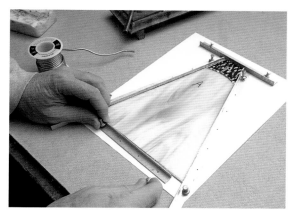

8 Finish soldering the seam with a rounded bead.

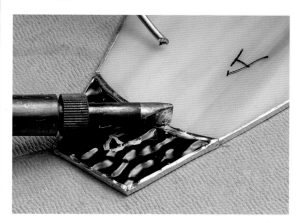

9 Turn over the glass and solder the back side in the same way.

10 Repeat steps 1–9 for the remaining seven sections.

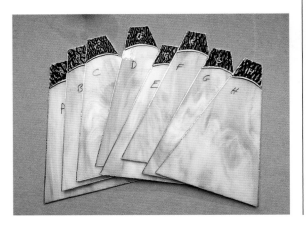

11 Using a little detergent on a towel, clean off the flux you applied to attach the top pieces.

12 Lay out the eight sections in a side-by-side, circular fashion, as shown, with about $1/16$ inch in between each. *Note:* The eight sections will not form a complete circle.

13 Plastic electrical tape is used to secure the glass as you tack-solder the cone. You will need seven 7-inch-long pieces of tape for the vertical sections.

14 Push a tape strip down the middle of each seam. It should be about 1 inch from the bottom and not cover the previously soldered rounded seam. Be careful not to move the glass sections as you tape them together.

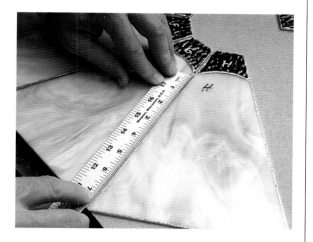

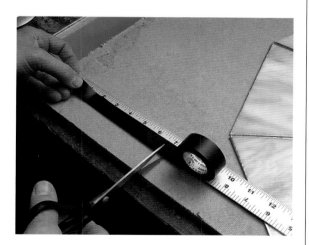

15 It's important that the cone stays together until you can get it tack-soldered, so you should tape around the glass sections as well. Starting at an upper point, overlap the tape about 1 inch and bend it around the eight sections, pressing the tape to the glass as you go. Cut the tape about $^1/_4$ inch from the end.

16 Attach a second piece of tape around the cone at the bottom. Start with a 1-inch overlap and cut the end about $^1/_4$ inch from the end.

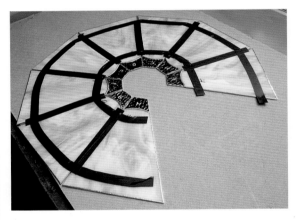

17 Apply flux at the bottom of all the vertical joints where two sections connect.

18 Apply flux at the top of the vertical joints.

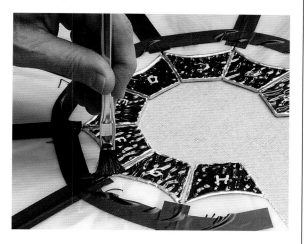

19 Apply flux at the same spots (top and bottom) on the outside of sections A and H.

20 From somewhere in the middle of the top opening, lift the taped unit off the surface, allowing the sections to form a cone.

21 With all the sections lined up to form an even cone, secure the cone in place by pressing down on the two tabs of tape.

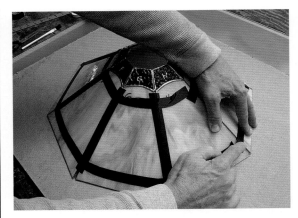

22 Hold the cone so that sections A and H sit evenly on the surface and the seam between A and H is even (one side doesn't stick out more than the other). Tack-solder at the bottom and top.

24 Tack-solder all the remaining sections at the top and bottom.

23 As you begin tack-soldering, you may have to adjust the sections slightly to ensure that they line up evenly. Again, be sure that one section doesn't stick out in front of its adjoining section. It's helpful to hold two sections in place as you solder.

Reinforcing the Cone

Although the cone is tack-soldered together, it's still not very sturdy. A reinforcing wire around the top opening and a brass cap will firm it up considerably.

1 From a spool of 14-gauge wire (12- or 16-gauge wire will also work), measure a length of wire around the cone plus a few inches.

2 Flux the wire as well as the top of the cone.

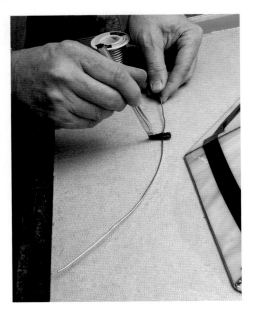

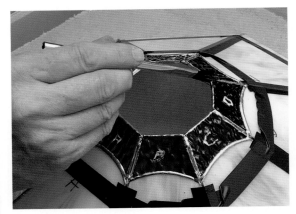

3 Position one end of the wire on the top edge of the glass at a joint, then tack-solder it there.

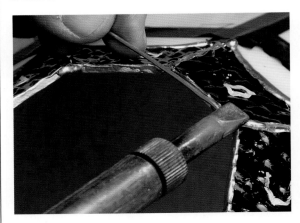

4 Use your iron to bend the wire at the next joint and tack-solder it in place.

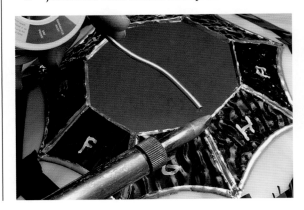

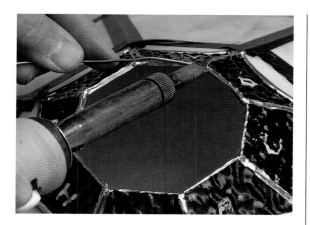

6 Rest your iron on the wire and finish attaching it by filling in the area between the wire and foil.

5 Complete the bending and tacking of the wire, cutting and tack-soldering it where it meets at the starting point.

Attaching the Lamp Cap

Lamp caps are typically made of brass, a rigid metal that accepts solder well. You should choose a cap with vent holes to allow heat from the lightbulb to escape. To determine the correct lamp cap size, measure the top opening from one angle to its opposite angle and round up to the next $1/2$ inch. For example, if the angle-to-angle measurement is $3\,3/4$ inches, you need a 4-inch cap. Measuring one side to the opposite side will result in too small of a size. We used a 4-inch cap for our lamp.

Lamp caps will generally have a layer of tarnish on them. You first need to remove this tarnish so the solder will flow smoothly.

1 With a ball of fine- to medium-grit steel wool, scour the cap until it is very bright.

2 Wipe off the cap and brush away any wool filings so they don't inadvertently get soldered to the cap.

3 Liberally flux the lamp cap. Starting at the top, melt solder onto the cap and move the iron in a circular pattern so the solder flows down. A little solder will go a long way. By keeping your iron on the cap the entire time, heat will be retained and the solder will flow evenly.

4 There may be areas on the cap where there is too much solder that is not flowing well; this is due to the flux evaporating. Simply reflux and remelt the areas using the same circular motion. Don't be concerned with the brown spots that are forming—this is only burned flux that will easily wash off later.

PRO TIP ✔

Use the top of a flux brush to hold and move the lamp cap as you solder. Do not touch it with your fingers—*it's extremely hot!*

5 Let the cap cool, then wash it in detergent.

6 It's important to center the cap in the cone's opening so the lamp will balance properly and hang evenly. Place the cap over the opening and inspect it from multiple views; adjust as necessary.

7 Flux at the eight connecting joints and tack-solder at any one joint to start.

8 To make sure that the cap is centered, carefully turn the cone upside down and inspect from the inside.

9 If the cap is off center, heat the soldered joint and lift the cap when the solder melts.

11 Inspect the cone from the underside again. When it is centered, attach at the other seven joints on the outside.

10 Move the cap so it is centered and reattach at one joint.

12 Lay the cone on its side, then flux and solder the inside seams.

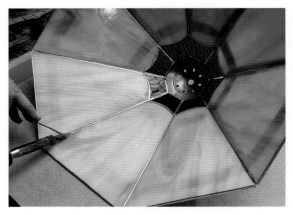

13 Apply solder at the cone's opening to cover the reinforcing wire and any exposed copper.

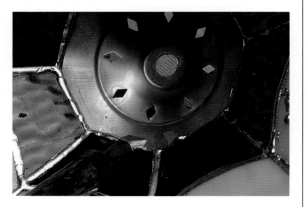

PRO TIP ✔

If there are any gaps in the glass where solder might run through, attach a piece of masking tape to the opposite side. This will catch the solder and make it easier to form a bead.

14 To further secure the lamp cap, melt solder from the reinforcement wire to the cap at the top of every other vertical seam. Allow your iron to rest on the wire and cap so the area heats up; this ensures a smooth and solid connection.

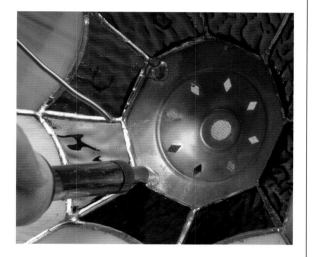

15 Carefully remove the electrical tape from the cone. Take off the horizontal pieces first, followed by the vertical strips. Be careful not to lift the edges of the copper foil.

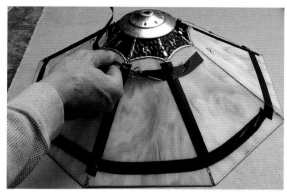

16 Position the cone exactly horizontal on a lamp leveler or in a cardboard box with newspaper for support. Apply flux to the seams.

PRO TIP ✔

The soldering process is greatly influenced by the laws of gravity. Soldering is easiest when done in a horizontal fashion as you would with a flat stained glass panel. Two methods for soldering a three-dimensional item will be illustrated.

- A lamp leveler allows you to change the lamp's position as you solder.

- A common cardboard box with crumpled newspaper is a suitable alternative.

17 First apply a flat coat of solder to fill each seam, then add a rounded bead coat of solder.

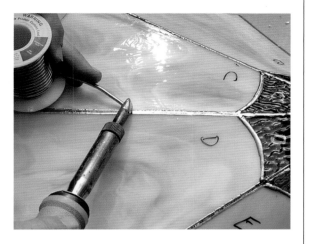

PRO TIP ✔

If you find that the solder is not flowing smoothly, copper is showing, or solder is spilling out onto the glass, you need more flux.

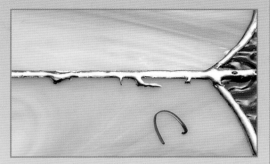

Apply flux on top of the solder and remelt. Add solder if necessary.

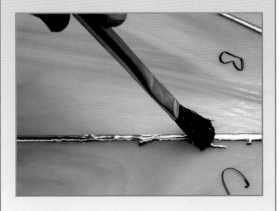

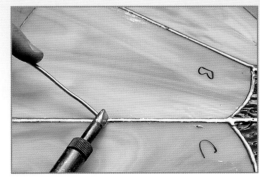

Constructing the Lampshade Band

The two band designs are labeled A and C on the pattern sheet. Because the solder seams separating the four pieces on each section of the band are intended to be parts of the leaves' stems, they must be attached in an alternating sequence (A, C, A, C, and so on) The skirt design sections B and D must alternate as well, starting with a B section under A, D under C, and so forth. These sequences are clearly illustrated below.

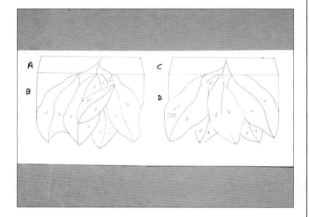

1 Measure the width of the band on the pattern sheet—it should be $1^1/4$ inches.

2 Determine the grain or pattern direction you want for your glass band and top of the cone.

3 Measure for cutting $1^1/4$-inch-wide strips.

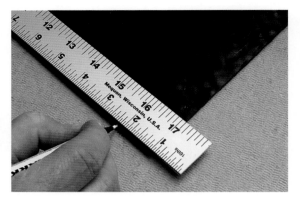

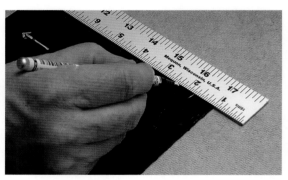

4 Use your ruler to line up the wheel of your cutter on the two marks you made. Score and break the glass. Cut a total of eight strips.

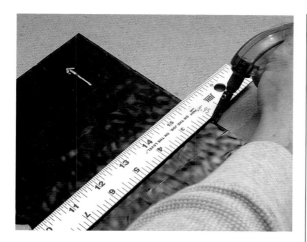

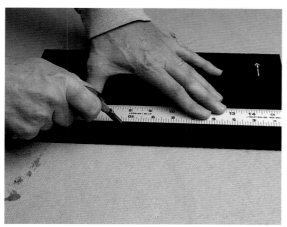

5 There will be four repeats of the band section marked A and four of the band section marked C. In order to keep the respective glass pieces together, designate the pieces in each section with a letter. We marked the four A sections A, B, C, and D. The four C sections are designated E, F, G, and H.

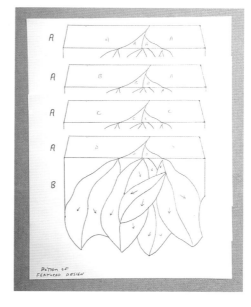

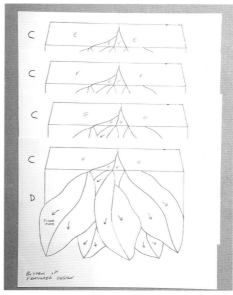

6 If you're using textured glass, remember to turn the paper pieces number-side-down so the glass texture will be on the outside of the lamp.

7 Use rubber cement to attach the paper patterns from each section onto a strip of glass, leaving approximately $1/4$ inch between pieces. The $1/4$-inch spacing will allow the pieces to be separated easily and the glass to break off cleanly.

8 Cut the glass pieces and grind them as needed. Assemble the pieces onto the pattern to check for proper fit. Wash and foil all the glass. Repeat for the other seven band sections.

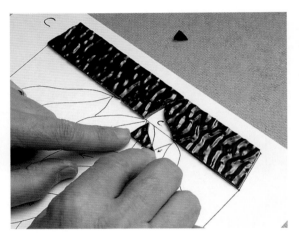

9 Attach a layout strip on the top of the pattern for band design A.

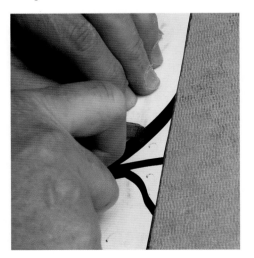

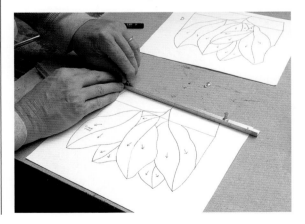

10 Attach layout strips on the left and right sides of the pattern.

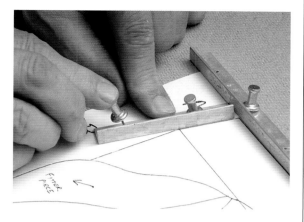

11 Insert the foiled glass pieces from one of your band design A sections, then attach a fourth layout strip to hold the section together.

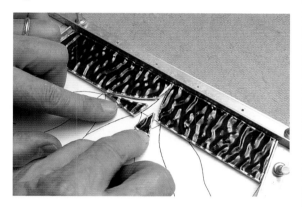

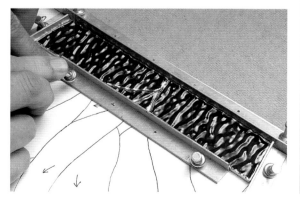

12 Apply flux to the copper seams and tack-solder the sections together.

13 Remove the lower layout strip and slide out the glass section. Finish soldering the front and back. Repeat this sequence for the remaining three A sections.

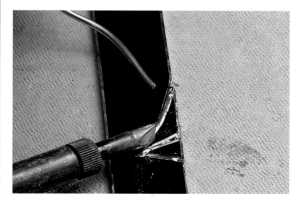

14 Attach layout strips to the pattern for band design C.

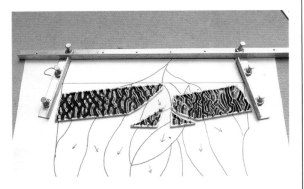

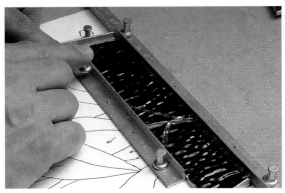

15 Solder the four C sections as you did for the A sections. Separate the A and C sections. It's easy to focus so intently on the mechanics of aligning and soldering sections that you forget to attach them in the right sequence. *Remember to alternate the A and C sections.*

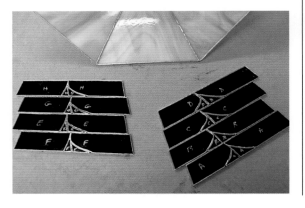

16 With the large cone resting on its side, apply flux on the edge where the band sections will be attached.

17 Apply flux to the shorter of the two long sides of the band sections.

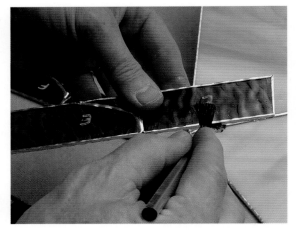

18 With an A section in your right hand and a C section in your left hand, hold them on the edge of the lamp cone. Tilt them up until the short adjoining sides are even with each other. This will establish the correct angle for all of the sections.

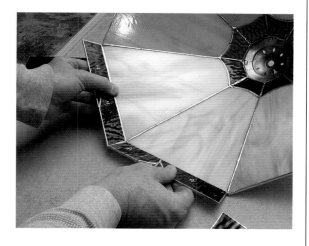

19 Remove the right A section and hold C in place. Tack-solder C to the cone at both ends.

20 Align an A section on the cone, then tack-solder in place on both ends.

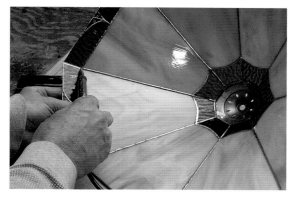

21 Push the two sections together so that their common inside corner is even along the seam. Tack-solder this seam.

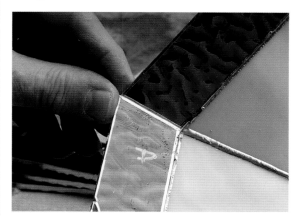

The cone will need to be supported to prevent it from rolling as you solder on new sections. Special foam blocks known as Wedgies are ideal because they will not burn, skid, or scratch the glass. A cardboard box with newspaper is a suitable alternative.

22 Tack-solder the six remaining band sections, remembering to alternate A and C sections. If you are using Wedgies or other outside supports, place them on either side of the cone. This will hold it steady as you attach each new section.

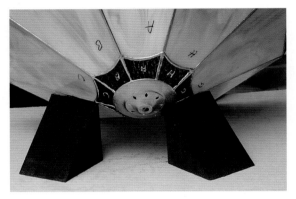

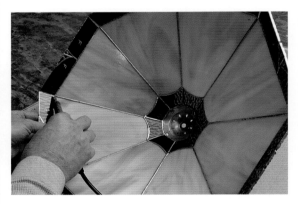

23 Position your supports so that the band sections rest flat on the work surface.

24 Still working from the inside of the lamp, solder the long seams between the cone and band sections and the short seams where the band sections are joined. *Remember to flux first!*

25 After you have finished soldering the inside of the shade, you will finish the outside seams. Reattach the cone to the lamp leveler or place it in the cardboard box. Position it so that the long seams are level. Remember: Do not try to fight gravity.

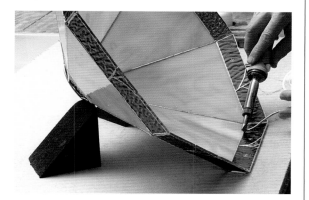

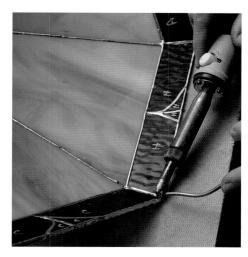

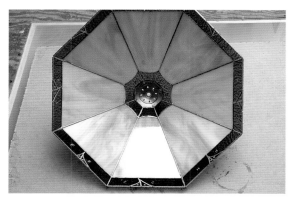

26 Flux the long seams and apply a bead of solder to each. *Note: As you complete one seam, wait at least five seconds before readjusting the lamp. This will give the solder time to harden.*

27 Readjust your shade and flux the short seams. Apply a beaded coat to the seams.

If you will not be ready to solder on the skirt sections for a day or more, wash off the remaining flux and dry thoroughly. Leaving the flux on for an extended period of time could cause some corrosion, which will make additional soldering considerably more difficult. If there is a chance that you will not solder for a week or two, put your shade in a black plastic trash bag after it's been cleaned; this will keep the solder seams from oxidizing.

Building the Lamp Skirt

The bottom sections that are attached to the lamp's middle band are referred to as the skirt. Your lamp has two different skirt designs (B and D), each of which is repeated alternately four times around the lamp. There is also a "fitter piece" that bridges both skirt designs B and D at an angle. The fitter piece was included in the design to blend the two leaf patterns without a vertical seam and add a sense of roundness to the shade.

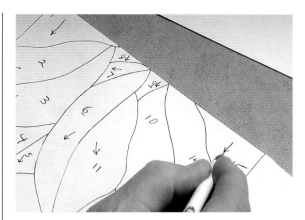

1 Starting with a copy of section B (this is the one with the fitter piece), number the pieces from 1 to 15. This will help you assemble the glass pieces after they have been cut and foiled.

2 Before you color-code your pattern sections, read page 116 on "Getting the Most from Your Glass."

3 Using colored pencils, designate the color of glass you have chosen for each piece by making a line on each pattern piece. After you cut apart the paper pattern, the resulting pile of pieces can be easily sorted by color. Repeat the same numbering and color-coding for four more sections of the B pattern. (Remember that one copy will be used to lay out your glass.)

4 Take a copy of the D pattern section and continue the numbering sequence starting with 16; this copy should end with 32. Color-code this section as well, then repeat the process for four additional copies.

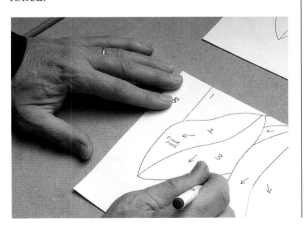

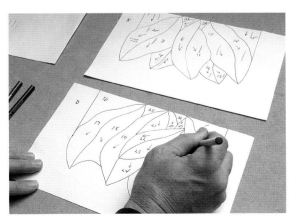

5 Use regular scissors to cut all the way around each of the eight pattern sections. (Remember to leave one copy of B and D intact for later.)

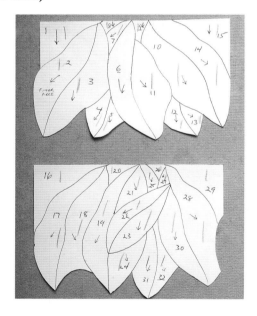

6 As each paper section is cut out, slight variations will result and pieces will not be interchangeable from section to section. To ensure that sections stay together throughout the soldering process, designate the four B sections as A, B, C, and D. Mark an A on all pieces of the A section and then repeat for B, C, and D.

7 The four D design sections should be designated as E, F, G, and H. Place an E on all pieces of the E section. Repeat this process for the F, G, and H sections.

8 Using your pattern shears, cut apart all pieces from the eight sections, being careful to keep the pieces in separate piles according to their letter designations.

GETTING THE MOST FROM YOUR GLASS

Whether you are planning to use one, two, three, or more colors for the leaves, hopefully you have chosen glass that will come alive with incandescent lightbulbs. You can determine this by holding your glass sheet a few inches away from a lightbulb. Do parts of the glass glow? Do the color variations mimic the look of a leaf? Does the light shine through in an even, pleasing way? Or does the color density of the glass block the light? Does too much transparency result in the bulb being seen? Are the glass colors solid without subtle variations within the sheet? All of these factors should be considered.

Ideally, you will choose glass using three criteria:

- **Color.** We used three different glasses for leaves in both our featured lamp and the lamp with alternative colors. In each lamp, the glass colors are in a similar family but different enough to provide some contrast.

- **Density.** In a lamp, the glass is enhanced when backlit from a lightbulb. A glass that does not let much light through should not be used for lamps. You will instead want to choose glass that glows when backlit but does not show the light fixture.

- **General interest.** This consideration can result in a stunning product versus one that is simply okay. Light green, medium green, and dark green glass might result in an okay lamp. Three shades of green, each with interesting striations and subtle color changes, will elevate a lampshade well beyond just okay.

GETTING THE MOST FROM YOUR GLASS

Nature will be an excellent guide as you choose areas of the glass for your leaves. Study the large leaf in the previous photo. Note the color variation and shadings. Study the vein patterns.

Also bear in mind that some areas of glass are simply too boring and should not be used. Your lamp has the potential to be a significant part of your stained glass legacy. Assuming it will be well built, it could last well beyond your lifetime. That being said, do not skimp on the glass. Be ready to buy plenty and possibly spend a little extra to get some especially nice sheets.

As you begin laying out your pattern pieces on the glass sheets, it's important to be able to backlight the glass so you can see how areas will actually look when the lamp is lit.

Notice the difference in the glass in the two photos. One is backlit using a light box. You can also use a lightbulb or place the glass on the ledge of a sunny window. If you are using multiple sheets within the same color family, designate each with a piece of masking tape marked with the colored pencils you used when marking your pattern. This will help you keep the colors straight.

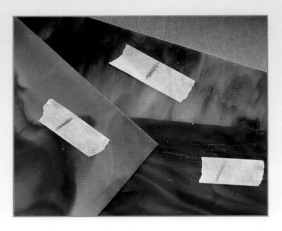

9 Starting with section A and using the patterns' directional arrows as a guide, carefully position pattern pieces on the glass, then attach them with rubber cement.

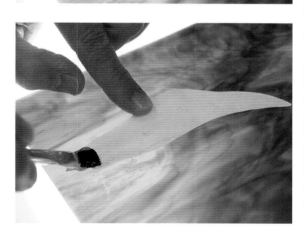

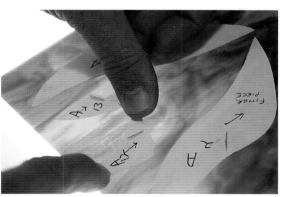

10 Separate the glass pieces from each sheet of glass you used and set them aside. Do the same for pattern sections B, C, and D.

11 Continuing with section E, affix the patterns to the glass with rubber cement. Cut the sections apart and set them aside. Do the same for sections F, G, and H.

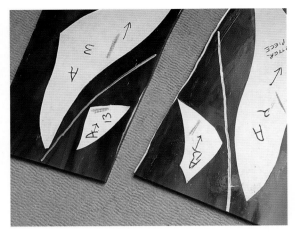

12 Again, starting with section A, cut apart the individual pieces on the glass. Try to leave at least ¹/₄ inch of glass around each piece.

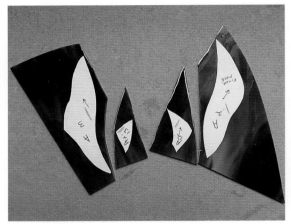

13 Search through your pieces and find the one that matches our piece number 3, as shown above. *Note: Your numbering sequence is probably different from ours.* The glass we used for piece number 3 is Kokomo 48, which is not a difficult glass to cut. The shape, however, has back-to-back inside curves as well as a pointed tip, making this one of the more difficult pieces to cut in the design.

14 Starting with the deepest of the inside curves, score along the pattern about halfway through the curve and graduate to the glass edge. Break out this piece.

15 Score the remaining half of the curve and break it out.

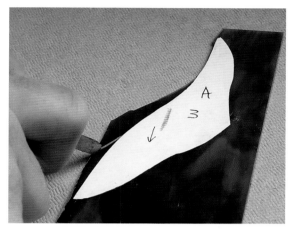

16 Score and break the remaining excess glass on the same side you've been cutting.

17 Score a relatively straight line on the opposite side of the previously removed curve. Break toward the point.

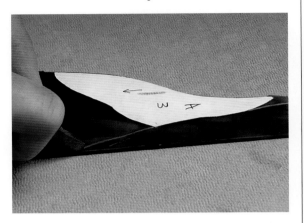

18 Score and break off the remaining glass attached to the point. Support the glass with your opposite hand so the point does not snap off.

19 Score another relatively straight line on the remaining side—running pliers will work well here.

20 Use breaking pliers to break the remaining side.

21 Groze any burrs or protruding areas that might still be present.

22 Cut the remaining pieces from section A and grind as necessary. Remember to grind right up to the pattern.

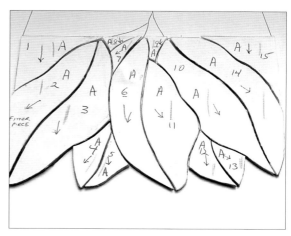

23 As you remove each paper pattern, write the corresponding number on the glass piece.

24 Cut the glass for the seven remaining skirt sections. Grind and wash all pieces.

25 Apply copper foil to all the pieces in section A. Attach layout strips to the top and right side of the pattern and assemble the glass pieces on top of the pattern. Remember that piece 22 (the fitter piece) protrudes past the left layout strip; remove it for later insertion.

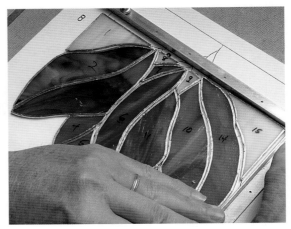

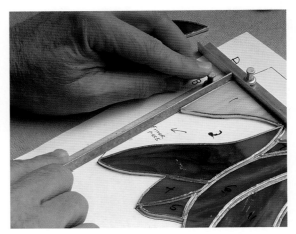

26 Attach the left layout strip. Put a few pushpins in the opening where the fitter piece will go in order to maintain proper spacing.

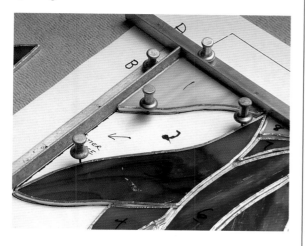

28 Flux and tack-solder section A together. Note: The top left corner piece barely touches the leaf piece on its right. Melt extra solder here for support; it will be removed later when the skirt is attached to the upper section of the lamp.

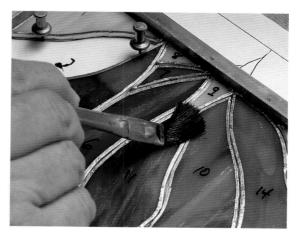

27 Place pushpins along the bottom of the design to prevent the pieces from moving.

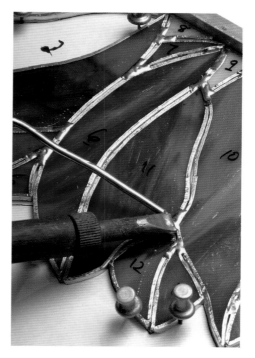

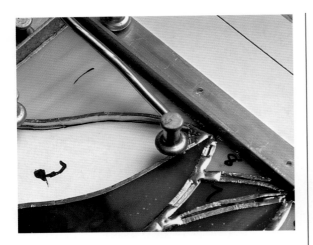

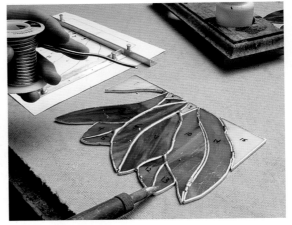

30 Finish soldering the front and back of section A.

29 Remove the bottom pushpins, then slide the section out and away from the layout strips.

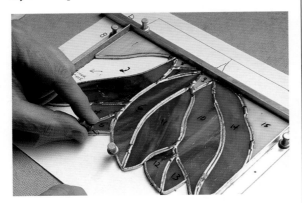

31 Write the letter A on the fitter piece for later reference.

32 Solder skirt sections B, C, and D in the same fashion as section A. Mark their respective fitter pieces as well.

33 Reassemble the layout strips on top of the other skirt pattern (design D). Position the glass pieces for section E and use push-pins to hold the pieces in place at the bottom.

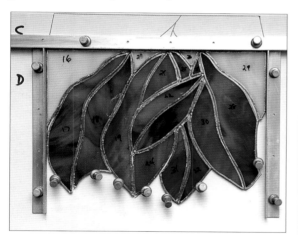

34 Flux and solder section E on the front and back. Assemble sections F, G, and H the same way.

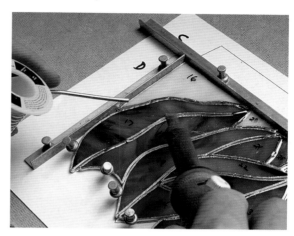

Attaching the Skirt

As you begin to attach the skirt sections to the bottom of the band sections, you must attach the B skirt sections to the A band sections and the D skirt sections to the C band sections. This is the way the original design was developed. If you are ignore this sequencing, you may end up having three sections tacked on before you realize your error. (This is what happened to us, and we had to reshoot some of the process.)

1 To help keep your glass sections organized, write a B on each of the B sections.

2 Write a D on each of the D glass sections.

3 Set the B sections on your left side and the D sections on your right for easy access.

4 Place the lamp cone in a cardboard box and support it all around with newspaper. Flux the entire rim.

5 You will be able to read the letter codes on the band sections from the inside of the lamp. Find a band section labeled with A, B, C, or D. For easy reference, write a B on the upper cone sections directly above the identified A band section. Write a D on the next section and alternate B and D for the other six sections.

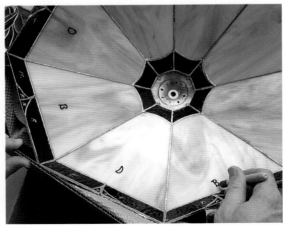

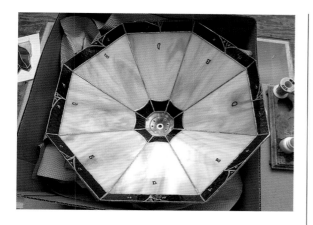

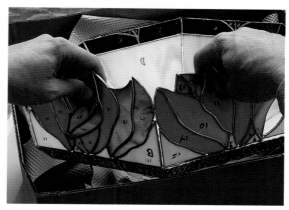

6 Set a D skirt section on top of the band where you have marked a D on the lamp cone. This starting point is critical because it sets the proper pattern for subsequent sections. Double-check that the stem seams on the band line up with the leaves on the skirt. Flux this seam as well as the two other vertical edges.

8 Remove the B section and, keeping the D section in place, tack-solder at several points along the seam on the outside of the lamp. If the section does not stand on its own, add a couple more solder tacks on the outside and inside.

7 Set a B section to the left of the D section. Raise the two sections until their common vertical sides touch evenly. The horizontal edges of sections B and D should rest on the edges of their adjoining band sections.

PRO TIP ✔

It's possible to carry small amounts of molten solder on your iron to areas that need to be tacked together. You will often find it helpful to hold the glass in place with one hand and solder with the other. To do this, you must first cool your iron in the wet sponge.

Then melt approximately 1/8 inch of solder onto the iron tip.

Carefully carry the solder to the point to be tacked. If it falls off before reaching its destination, cool the iron tip and try again.

9 Flux the bottom and the sides of the B section and set it in place, again making sure that the horizontal edge matches up with the edge on the band. Tack-solder section B to the band at both ends and in the middle.

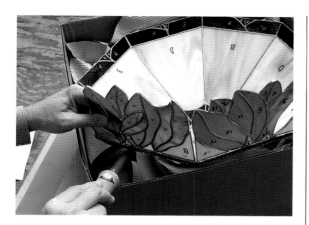

11 Flux another D section and attach it to the left of the B section.

10 Push the two sections together so the seam where they meet is even. Hold the sections in place and tack-solder.

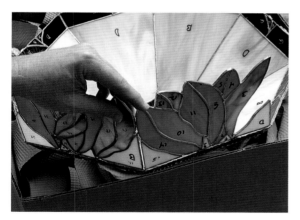

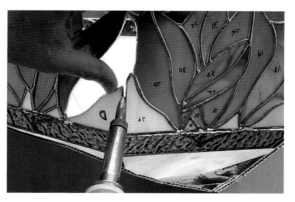

You must now add the fitter pieces that were removed earlier. When you soldered the D sections, we recommended that you build up the solder where the fitter piece was missing. This needs to be removed so the fitter piece will fit.

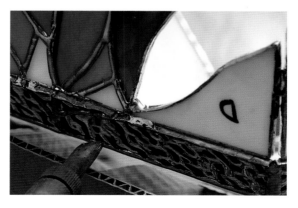

12 Flux the area. Melt the solder and pull it toward you.

13 Try the fitter piece in the opening. It will not yet fit perfectly, but you'll want it to be close. Because you are putting a straight piece of glass across a curved span, it will not sit evenly on all the glass it touches. The fitter piece will touch the band and the opposite point will touch the leaf on the adjoining section. The other points of contact will vary, so do not be concerned. Move the piece around until you find where it fits the best.

14 Tack-solder the fitter piece at several points.

15 Tack-solder another B section and continue in the same sequence until all eight skirt sections are attached and the fitter pieces are inserted.

16 If you run into a fitter piece that is too large for the opening, remove the foil and place it in the opening. Use a marker to indicate areas that need to be ground off.

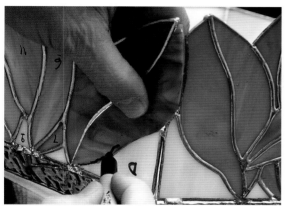

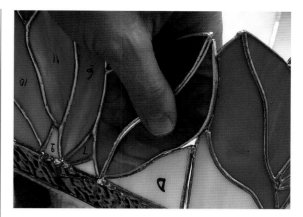

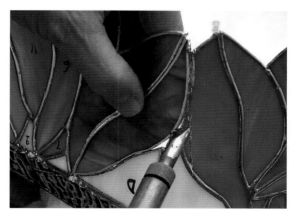

17 Grind a little at a time until you have a suitable fit. Foil and solder the fitter piece into place.

18 Because the lamp can be balanced on a skirt section with the use of two wedgies or other supports, you should solder the inside of the lamp first. Position the lamp so it sits flat on a skirt section, then position two Wedgies on the back side.

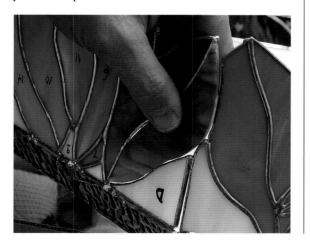

19 Solder the seams connecting the leaves, the seam that connects the skirt to the band, and all around each fitter piece. You're aiming for a beaded edge. Remember to use masking tape to prevent solder from running through areas where you may have some space.

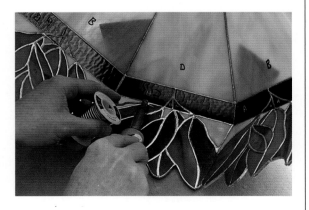

20 Reposition the shade on a new skirt section and be sure the wedgies or other supports are securely supporting the shade. Complete all inside soldering.

21 For the outside soldering, you can use the cardboard box filled with newspaper or a lamp gig. Position the shade in the box or on the jig so a skirt section is horizontal to your table. Remember not to fight gravity.

22 Solder the eight horizontal skirt band seams.

23 Solder the vertical seams that connect the skirt sections.

24 Solder any remaining seams around the fitter pieces.

25 Inspect the outside and inside of the shade for any problems.

PRO TIP ✔

You will often find some solder blemishes on the inside of your shade. Solder can drip through the lampshade from above and splatter on the section below.

Blobs can occur where solder melts from above but does but go all the way through. When this happens, apply flux and drag the iron along the seam so it evens out.

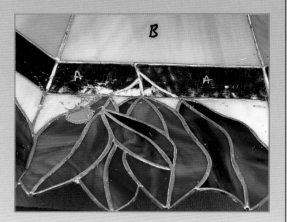

Sometimes the solder can be lifted with a fingernail or craft knife if it has not bonded with the solder below.

Attaching the Bottom Reinforcement Wire

There is a natural tendency for a lamp to want to pull apart from above and from side to side. Gravity is still at work even when the soldering is complete. The forces from above were neutralized when you reinforced the top of the lamp cap and also soldered it on the inside. The side-to-side forces will be mitigated by soldering a wire around the lamp's perimeter.

Since the lamp has such an irregularly shaped bottom edge, you'll want to use a wire that bends easily around the leaves and into the crevices. Twenty-gauge wire will work fine, but anything larger will be difficult to bend.

This is a good time to change to a $^1/_4$-inch or smaller soldering iron tip if you have one.

1 Unravel a length of tinned copper wire that will encircle the lamp, then add at least another foot for the ups and downs.

2 The wire will work much better if it's straight. Place one end in a vise or secure it in some other fashion such as by wrapping it around a nail or post. Using your grozing pliers, pull the wire from the opposite end until it straightens.

3 Flux the shade all around the perimeter, covering both the outside and inside edges.

4 Flux the wire as well.

5 Start by tacking one end of the wire into one of the crevices between two skirt sections. The wire should be centered on the bottom edge of the glass.

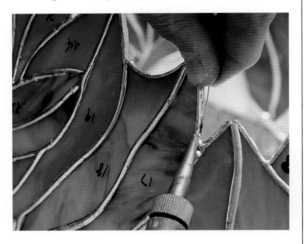

6 Pull on the wire and tack it an inch or so from the first tack. Bending the wire will be easier if you keep solder away from the points.

PRO TIP ✔

Since copper wire conducts considerable heat, keep your fingers at least an inch from the point of contact. If it starts to feel warm, the heat is coming.

7 Continue to bend the wire and tack it every inch or so. The wire should be flat against the entire edge.

8 When you get back to where you started, use wire cutters to snip the wire.

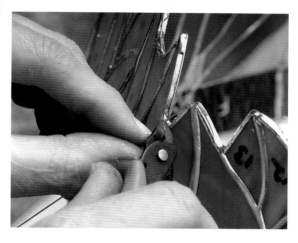

9 Push the last wire section into the crevice with your knife and solder it.

building a stained glass lampshade • **137**

10 Place the lampshade back in the cardboard box and begin filling in spaces around the wire with solder. You will need to level the shade frequently so you can solder a horizontal section. You will only be able to do about one inch at a time.

11 The objective is to render a smooth and slightly rounded bottom edge. You will be able to bead the solder only to the height of the wire. If solder bulges past the edges of the glass or drips over the edge, you are using too much. If the solder blobs up in spots, apply a little flux and smooth again. After you have finished soldering the bottom edge, set the shade on end and support it in the box or with Wedgies. You now want to cover any foil that is still exposed.

12 Tin the inside and outside edges, then make any other alterations that may be needed.

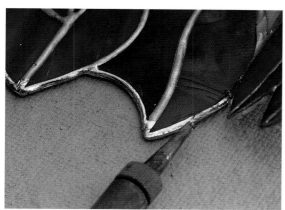

Finishing the Shade

The shade is nearly finished, and it's okay to step back and admire your work. A few finishing touches will make it look even better. Be patient!

1 You should first clean the lamp thoroughly with a mild detergent (we use a product called Simple Green). There is probably an ounce or two of flux, glue, and other residue to remove in addition to all the letter and number markings. If the markings do not come off with the sponge, use a nylon scrubber to go over the marks lightly.

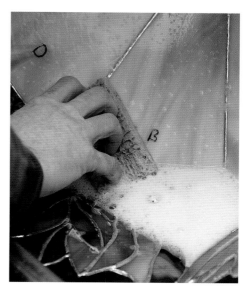

2 Rinse and dry the shade.

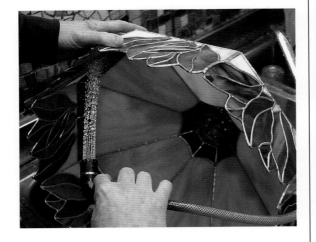

3 Spray the shade liberally with a flux remover and buff it dry.

4 While wearing rubber gloves, use a soft sponge (we use old carpet padding) to apply a liberal amount of patina to all of the solder.

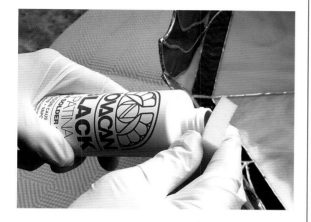

5 After about 5 minutes, rinse the shade with warm water to remove the excess patina.

6 Go over the shade lightly with a sponge and the same detergent used in step 1. Do not scrub too hard as you might abrade some of the patina. Rinse again in warm water and dry.

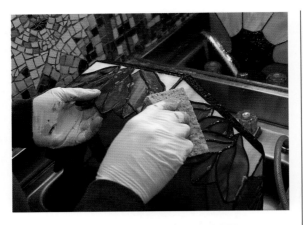

8 The last step in the process is to use a finishing wax to make the patina and glass shine. Using a soft cloth and a squirt or two of wax, spread the wax over the entire lamp.

7 Spray liberally with the flux remover (which is also a patina remover) and buff dry.

9 Allow the wax to dry to a haze (this will take 10 to 20 minutes). Buff all the solder seams and glass to a bright shine.

Your shade is now finished. The next step is to light it up!

FINISHING THE PROJECT

- ☐ Clean project with a nontoxic, all-purpose cleaner. Rinse and dry.

- ☐ Spray liberally with flux/patina cleaner. Buff and dry.

- ☐ Apply patina with soft sponge.

- ☐ Rinse off the patina.

- ☐ Spray liberally with flux/patina cleaner. Buff and dry.

- ☐ Apply finishing wax. Buff to a bright shine with a soft cloth.

PRO TIP ✔

Occasionally, some areas on different metals will not completely take the color of the patina. This sometimes happens on solder and more frequently on brass, lead, and zinc. Should this occur, rub the affected area with steel wool and apply additional patina. Wipe off the excess, clean with flux/patina cleaner, and shine with wax.

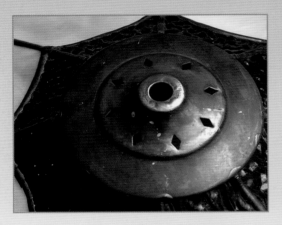

Electrifying the Lampshade

The size of your lampshade makes it suitable to display on a large table base or floor stand or even hang over a bar or table.

If you are using it on a floor stand, make sure the bottom of the base is heavy enough to support the shade (many reproduction bases for stained glass lamps have extra weights concealed under the bottom). The floor base shown in the photo at left is 52 inches high with a 12-inch base. If the shade is to be hung, the easiest way to electrify it is to use a three-bulb socket cluster. By using three bulbs, the light will be distributed equally around the shade, eliminating one "hot spot" in the middle. We used 60-watt bulbs, but other wattage bulbs will also work.

Three-bulb socket clusters come prewired and are available in most stained glass supply shops. You will also need a lamp chain and a loop.

Thread the wire through the hole in the loop, then thread the loop onto the top of the socket fixture.

2

1 Installation is very easy. Insert the lamp cord through the bottom of the lamp cap and pull the cord from the top until the fixture is flush with the underside of the cap.

3 Because your shade is relatively heavy, you should choose a 9- or 11-gauge chain for hanging. Attach one chain link over the loop and close with pliers. The opposite end will hang from the ceiling attachment.

If you're like most people, you're anxious to see what the shade looks like when lit. Use a temporary plug and light it up. Stand back and take in the moment. Your hard work will hopefully have paid off.

7

Basic Stained
Glass Repair

Of THE HUNDREDS OF LAMPS BUILT IN OUR studio over the past twenty-four years, several have developed a broken piece or two before going to their new homes. I personally have broken a couple on our metal wash sink, dropped a hanging loop on one, let one slip out of my hands while packing, and bumped one with the pliers while closing the chain link; several others can most likely be attributed to heat during soldering. Although discovering a broken piece in a "finished" lamp is irksome, it is certainly not the end of the world.

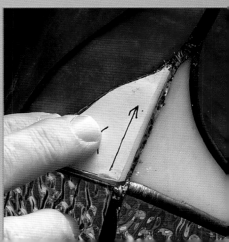

1 Working on the outside of the lamp, use steel wool to scratch off most of the patina that surrounds the broken piece.

2 Scratch off the patina on the inside as well.

3 Working from the inside, draw a grid that resembles a tic-tac-toe design on the broken piece. Also draw short lines from any corners (this piece has three corners).

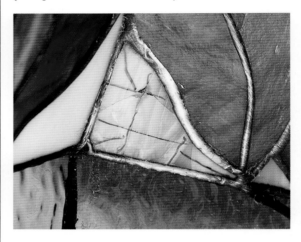

4 Score all the lines.

5 From the outside of the lamp, tap the score lines with the brass screw on your glass cutter or the ball of a conventional cutter.

6 Keep tapping until the center piece of glass falls out of the hole. When you have discovered the right force, about ten taps should be sufficient.

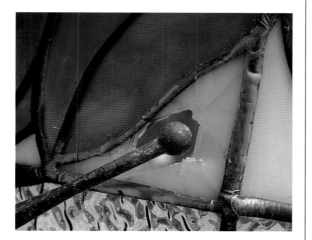

7 Flux the solder around the broken piece

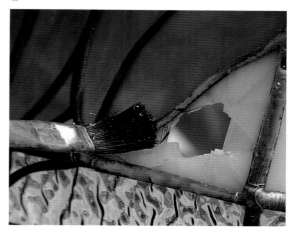

PRO TIP ✔

When removing a broken piece, particularly if it is fairly small, you will find that switching to a small iron tip ($1/8$ to $1/4$ inch) will be helpful.

8 Melt off most of the solder surrounding the broken piece by allowing it to flow down the seams and away from the piece.

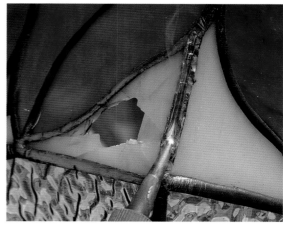

10 Gently pull the piece loose from the foil.

9 With needle-nose pliers, hold a piece of glass that has one edge soldered to the lamp. Melt the area where the piece is attached, moving the iron back and forth until the solder is molten.

11 Continue around the opening and remove the broken pieces one at a time.

12 When all of the glass is removed, search for the seam on the foil that was around the broken piece. Melt the solder at the seam and, as it melts, free up one end of the foil by raising it with your soldering iron tip.

13 Take hold of the raised foil end with the needle-nose pliers. Melt the solder at that spot and gently pull the foil loose as the solder continues to melt.

14 Move your iron along the seam and continue pulling the foil loose as you melt the solder. Be careful not to pull the foil from the adjoining pieces loose.

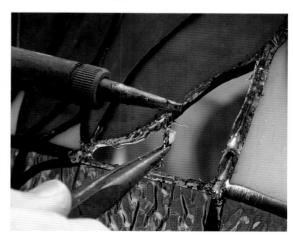

16 Cut out a paper pattern to match the broken piece.

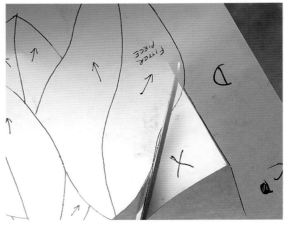

15 Flux the opening and clean out the remaining solder as best you can.

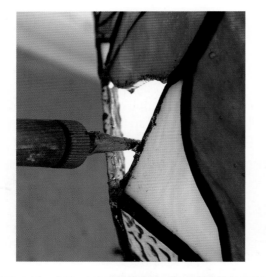

17 Mark the direction of the glass grain.

25   Cover the new solder with patina.

26   Wipe off the patina.

27   Clean and wax the area.

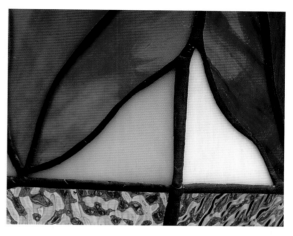

Once you have done a few repairs, a job like this one takes only 15 to 20 minutes.

8

Stained Glass Lamp Gallery

Graceful Flowers

Designed and fabricated by Nan Maund

The Carter Pub Lantern
Rainbow Vision Stained Glass

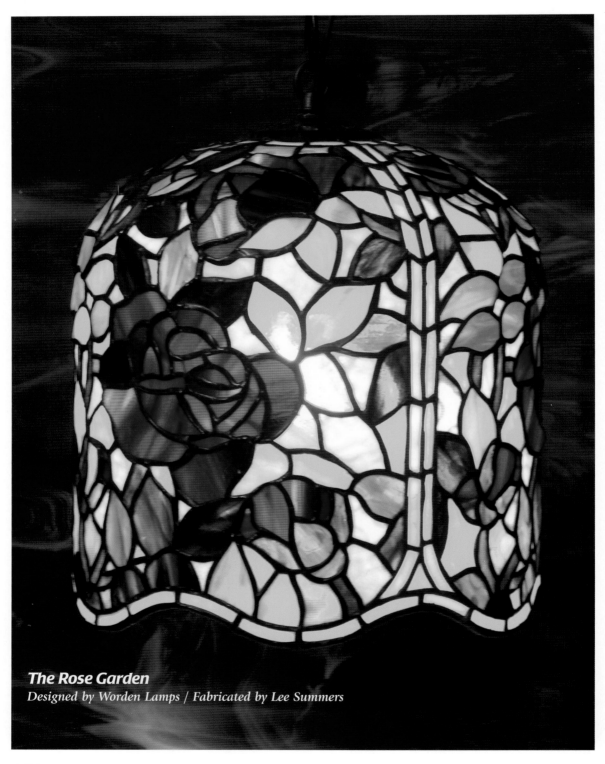

The Rose Garden
Designed by Worden Lamps / Fabricated by Lee Summers

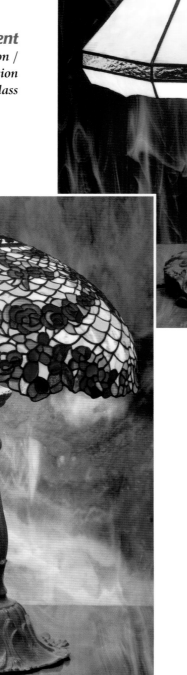

Parlor Accent

Designed by Craig Johnston /
Fabricated by Rainbow Vision
Stained Glass

Rose Garland

Designed by Worden Lamps /
Fabricated by Lee Summers

A Nice Beginning
From Basic Stained Glass Making
(Stackpole Books, 2003)

Ceiling Splendor
Designed and fabricated by
Lynn Haunstein

The Ashley Blues
Rainbow Vision Stained Glass

The Brady Eight
Rainbow Vision Stained Glass

The Conner Illusion
Rainbow Vision Stained Glass

The Jackson
Rainbow Vision Stained Glass

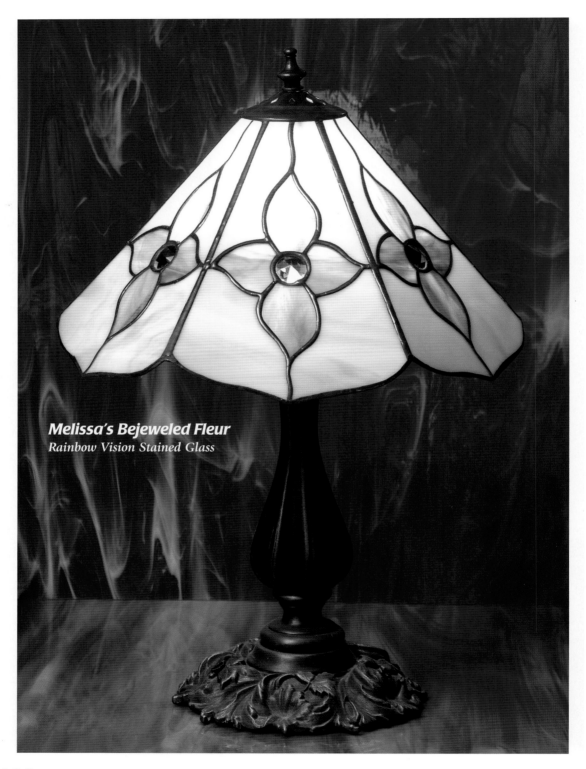

Melissa's Bejeweled Fleur
Rainbow Vision Stained Glass

18-inch Peony
Designed by Odyssey Lamps /
Fabricated by Hugh Archer

Choosing a Suitable Lamp Base

There is a wide range of lamp bases available for all of the shades in the gallery. Some are very ornate, others rather plain, and many in the middle. Bases are available as short as 5 inches and range up to 30 inches for table bases and 72 inches for floor bases. We offer a few guidelines for selecting an appropriate base:

- The width of the bottom of the lamp base should be somewhere between 40 percent and 50 percent of the shade's diameter. A shade with a 16-inch diameter will look good on bases 7 to 8 inches wide.

- The base height is generally measured from the bottom of the light socket to the bottom of the base. A good base height should be a little more than the height of the shade. An 8-inch high shade looks best on a base 9-inch or higher.

- The harp on the base should be about the same size as the height of the shade. This allows the shade's bottom to be about even (or a little below) the bottom of the socket. An 8-inch shade looks best on a $7^1/2$- to 8-inch harp.

- Bases come in different finishes. Try to match the finish on your shade to the finish on your base.

Books

Cooper, Suzanne. *Simply Lamps.* Spring Branch, TX: Susanne Cooper Inc., 1994.

Doran, Lucinda, and Brian McMillan. *Elegant Lamps.* Winnipeg, Canada: Walrus Publications, 2000.

Haebich, Scott. *Prairie Style Lampshades and Lanterns.* Grand Rapids, MI: SGN Publishing, 1995.

Wardell, Randy, and Judy Huffman. *More Lampshade Patterns II.* Fort Lauderdale, FL: Wardell Publications, Inc., 1986.

Online

Glastar Corp.
20721 Marilla Street
Chatsworth, CA 91311
800-423-5635
www.glastar.com
Manufacturer of glass grinders and other stained glass tools. This site includes lots of glass-related topics.

Inland Craft Products, Co.
32052 Edward Drive
Madison Heights, MI 48071
800-521-8428
www.inlandcraft.com
Carries glass grinders and other equipment used in stained glass. Also includes a handy state-by-state locator of stained glass supply stores.

Kokomo Opalescent Glass
1310 South Market Street
Kokomo, IN 46904-2265
765-457-8136
www.kog.com
The oldest glass manufacturer in the country, established in 1888. Take a virtual tour of the factory, click on their sample set, and see products from their hot glass studio.

Odyssey Lamps
8317 Secura Way
Santa Fe Springs, CA 90670
800-403-1981
www.odysseylamps.com
Website shows the many molds and patterns available, as well as prices and other interesting information.

Rainbow Vision Stained Glass
3105 Walnut Street
Harrisburg, PA 17109
800-762-9309
www.rainbowvisionsg.com
Contains information about all things stained glass; equipment and materials available for purchase.

Retailers of Art Glass and Supplies (RAGS)
www.stainedglassretailers.com
A nonprofit organization of owners of retail stores selling stained glass supplies around the world. Includes good information about the craft, as well as listings of supplier locations.

Spectrum Glass
24105 Sno-Woodinville Road
Woodinville, WA 98072
425-483-6699
www.spectrumglass.com
This site is loaded with technical information, sample colors, free patterns, and much more.

Uroboros Glass
2139 North Kerby Avenue
Portland, OR 97227
503-284-4900
www.uroboros.com
This site includes details about the factory and glass samples.

Wissmach Glass, Co.
420 Stephen Street
Paden City, WV 26159
304-337-2253
www.wissmachglass.com
This site has factory information, glass samples, and a gallery.

Worden Lamps
P.O. Box 519
Granger, WA 98932
800-541-1103
www.wordensystem.com
Website displays the many molds and patterns available and other related products.

Youghiogheny Glass
900 West Crawford Avenue
Connellsville, PA 15425
724-628-0332
www.youghioghenyglass.com
Established in 1978, this company specializes in Tiffany reproduction glass. Website includes sample sets, gallery, and factory information.